WORLD WAR II LIBRARY

For the hundreds of thousands of readers fascinated by World War II history, Dell has created the World War II Library—outstanding nonfiction narratives that convey the total experience of war with historical accuracy and detailed immediacy that until now could be understood only by those who had fought it.

BATTLE OF THE HEDGEROWS

We were being annihilated, our ranks disintegrating as we ran. Glancing at my comrades around and behind me to draw courage and strength from their presence, I saw that the field was being littered with dead, our dead. A trooper in front of and to the right of me was hit in the chest by an 88 shell. His body disappeared from the waist up, his legs and hips with belt, canteen and entrenching tool still on taking three more steps, then falling. Another trooper went to his knees, ran a couple of yards in that position, tried to gain his feet, stumbled and went down. . . . Other men were falling, but at the same time others had gained the hedge and were lobbing grenades over it. We had been yelling and screaming like animals at the top of our lungs all the way. The Germans were falling back. . . .

Also by Donald R. Burgett

Seven Roads to Hell
The Road to Arnhem
Beyond the Rhine

CURRAHEE!

A Screaming Eagle
at Normandy

DONALD R.
BURGETT

Foreword by Stephen E. Ambrose
Introduction by Martin Blumenson

A DELL BOOK

A Dell Book
Published by
Dell Publishing
A division of Random House, Inc.
1540 Broadway
New York, New York 10036

Cover design Gerald Pfeifer
Cover photo Mark Bando

Dell books may be purchased for business or promotional use or for
special sales. For information please write to: Special Markets
Department, Random House, Inc., 1540 Broadway,
New York, N.Y. 10036

Dell® is a registered trademark of Random House, Inc., and the
colophon is a trademark of Random House, Inc.

ISBN: 0-440-23630-4

Reprinted by arrangement with Presidio Press

Printed in the United States of America

Published simultaneously in Canada

September 2000

10 9 8 7 6 5 4

OPM

To the men of the 506th Regiment, 101st Airborne Division, some of whom I knew and some of whom I did not, many of whose acts of bravery will never be known, and especially to those who made the supreme sacrifice, I would like to dedicate this story, this bit of history.

CONTENTS

FOREWORD

The junior officers and enlisted men were the real heroes
of World War II. Wherever they went they brought libera-
tion, freedom, and democracy. That this is so can be
learned from any Frenchman, Italian, Belgian, German,
any Korean, Japanese, Chinese—the GIs meant cigarettes,
candy, K rations, and liberty. The truth is exemplified in
Currahee! by an eighteen-year-old American paratrooper
who never bothered to think about the causes or con-
sequences of war, but who fought it magnificently.

Donald Burgett enlisted in the army in 1943, just out of
high school, and volunteered for the paratroopers. He went
into Company A of the 101st Airborne Division and was put
through as rigorous a training program as any soldier in the
world, much of which he describes in a matter-of-fact manner. Then it was off to England for the final preparation,
then the long agonizing wait for loading up and taking off
for Normandy.

His personal equipment consisted of: one suit of O.D.s,
which he wore under his jump suit, helmet, boots, gloves,

main chute, reserve chute, Mae West, and M1 rifle, a .45 automatic pistol, trench knife, jump knife, hunting knife, machete, one cartridge belt, two bandoleers, two cans of machine gun ammo totaling 676 rounds of .30 ammo, 66 rounds of .45 ammo, one Hawkins mine capable of blowing the track off a tank, four blocks of TNT, one entrenching tool, three first-aid kits, two morphine needles, one gas mask, a canteen of water, three days' supply of K rations, two days' supply of D rations, six fragmentation grenades, one Gammon grenade, two smoke grenades, one orange panel, one blanket, one raincoat, one change of socks and underwear, two cartons of cigarettes, "and a few other odds and ends." In twelve days of combat he used every item— although he never changed clothes.

Burgett writes with an unforgiving honesty. He never says so but it is clear that there is nothing like it: nothing in civilian life, nothing in the peace-time army, can remotely compare to the fear or the physical demands. Here is a sample (and a mild one): "Running across the fields I came upon a young German paratrooper lying belly down and firing a burp gun in our general direction. As he saw me his eyes became round with fear. He rolled onto his right side, swinging his weapon with the same movement and squirting a long string of fire. The bullets crackled past my ears just as I shot him through the head."

Here is a passage that sounds like it came from World War I—but actually it is Normandy, 1944. Burgett was sent to the rear with a message. The dead were every-where. "Finally I took to stepping from body to body as if they were stepping stones in a river of gore. The bodies were so bloated that occasionally they gave out noises that sounded like groans. This gave me quite a start and made me look around wildly to see if one of the mutilated things was rising up. It seems hard to believe but I walked for about a quarter of a mile stepping from body to body."

There is much more in this outstanding book. I have read a lot of books on the experience of combat from both World Wars, and this is by a longshot the best. Without qualification.

—*Stephen E. Ambrose*

INTRODUCTION*

The capacity of the human spirit to absorb shock is miraculous. A man can be twisted almost beyond recognition, driven to the edge of insanity, tormented by the fires of hell; he can suffer adversity, pain and cruelty, undergo degradation—yet retain the sensibilities and compassion of a human being.

Take the case of Donald R. Burgett. Put into uniform at the age of 18, brutalized, turned loose with a group of similarly oriented youngsters, he was, in naked terms, a killer. That he was part of a regularly constituted military force, trained and committed according to the laws of warfare to engage and defeat the enemy, is almost beside the point. Burgett and the paratroopers he served with in World War II, along with the Rangers, the Marines, and the combat infantrymen, participated in a cold-blooded orgy of destruction. They had to. Not only to win, but to

* This introduction was written for the original edition of *Currahee!*, published in 1967.

survive on the battlefield. Even then, they had no certainty, only a better chance, of emerging unharmed.

The rules were simple; operate with automatic efficiency as the result of a deliberate process of manipulation that has deadened the senses and the mind; give no quarter in a murderous game of hide-and-seek, for the enemy is trained and motivated precisely in the same manner; and come to regard the deaths of others with the virtual disinterest of an animal. Divested of bugles and parades, of high-minded rationale, of patriotism and glory, of the moral questions, stripped to its rude essentials, combat for the individual soldier is a nightmare—crazy things done by crazy men in a crazy world—pervaded by incessant and suppressed fear.

Yet the chaos could only submerge temporarily, not extinguish the demands of human dignity—the pangs of shame, remorse, and guilt. What does Burgett do after describing how he shot his first Germans? He says he doesn't know whether he really hit them—they were some distance away and they would have fallen even if the bullets had only come close. The fate of the prisoners he saw being marched toward the enemy lines, the moans he heard from the disfigured who pled for mercy sickened him. His pain and his protest, though invisible and muted, are present on almost every page.

Revealing the honest viewpoint of the "dogface" soldier, Burgett had no interest in the issues of the war, the management of the military resources, the historical context of the conflict. He found himself in a seemingly disordered and bewildering barracks world, which required an unthinking submission to all the conditions imposed. Basic training, particularly for paratroopers, was shock treatment. A recruit had to prove his toughness—be tough enough to take it, tough enough to stand up, tough enough to be a man. His previous life became unreal; his future dissolved and became non-existent. Only the present was important, and whatever made the present more bearable was acceptable. Taking on a protective callousness, disoriented from civilian concerns, his prior morality disjointed, his humor dislocated, he came to view all as merely transient—friendship and even life itself. He was then ready for the battlefield and the need to kill in an impersonal manner. All of this Burgett candidly presents and perhaps unknowingly understands as necessary to retain a semblance of sanity in a house of bedlam.

Instinctively authentic, Burgett's narrative describes how men learned the risky business of jumping from airplanes, how they parachuted into Normandy to open the invasion of northwest Europe, and how they fought. It shows the meaning of morale, discipline, and leadership. It reveals a soldier's attitudes toward his comrades, his superiors, his enemies and his own existence. But above all, it is a study in horror—madness has become normal—juxtaposed with tenderness. It begins with the dehumanizing effect of training, which succeeded superbly in preparing men for battle; continues through the waiting, the transition through which Burgett and other youngsters passed on their way to the final test; goes on through combat; and has no end even in the immediate aftermath—which makes this account of World War II relevant in these days of Vietnam.

Mild-mannered, soft-spoken, even today somewhat shy,

Burgett seems to have emerged from the war unscathed. There is no trace of the soldier who fought across Europe from Normandy through Austria and who received three wounds and the Bronze Star Medal for Valor. Discharged from Camp Atterbury, Indiana, on the last day of 1945, he was, as he says, lucky enough to catch a plane ride home to Detroit. On that New Year's Eve, when he tried to buy a beer in a neighborhood bar, he couldn't get served. He was too young.

Restless, he was unable to settle down. He worked on several construction jobs, took flight training on the GI bill, earned his pilot's license and headed for Alaska to homestead. He got as far as California. But he missed the woods and waters, the hunting and fishing of Michigan. He returned, became a roofer, married, and accepted the responsibilities and routines of family life.

From the time he left the Army, he talked constantly of the war, trying, no doubt, to understand the meaning of the greatest single adventure of his life. A friend suggested he put it all down on paper, and it seemed like a good idea. His children would then know what he had done. The achievements of the paratroopers he had so proudly served with would be preserved. And perhaps he would finally get the war out of his system.

Using his regimental history as a guidepost for dates and places, referring occasionally to letters he had sent home, consulting a miscellaneous collection of newspaper clippings he had saved, he discovered he had almost total recall. He had always sketched pictures, and this practice, he found, had given him the habit of perceiving and retaining details of scenes he might otherwise have forgotten.

He started with pencil, then shifted to typewriter, and after writing nights and weekends for more than four years, he produced a story that is both personal and universal, immediate and enduring. Simply written, matter of fact in tone, it has primitive power and a direct outlook; it is alarmingly ingenuous.

There is no talk of why he and his companions accepted the dangers and difficulties, but the explanations are implicit throughout. The reasons for being at war? No need to articulate or discuss them. They were clearly understood. And valid. Their leaders? All great men. President Roosevelt, General Eisenhower, and Prime Minister Churchill were as real and as vital as Colonel Bob Sink, General Maxwell Taylor and Captain Davis; all generated inspiration, confidence, trust and love. Morale? Great. Members of an elite outfit, they had self-esteem. They were unbeatable. They had worked hard to "blouse our pant legs in the tops of our boots" and this was an honor of tremendous significance. And finally, there was the exhilaration, the sheer joy of being caught up in something grand and noble and worth the peril of death.

Whether all the incidents are real in an absolute sense is unimportant. This is the way Burgett saw them, heard about them, dreamed of them or remembered them, and his point of view reflects that of the average GI. The dead Japanese officer, for example, that Burgett says he saw in Normandy and the others that his buddies reported seeing: Burgett probably never knew what a Japanese uniform looked like. He probably came across a Russian of Mongoloid features, a Tatar perhaps, a member of one of the groups from Eastern Europe—usually called *Ost* battalions—that fought alongside the Germans in France. Thus too the Hungarians taken prisoner; they might have belonged to an *Ost* unit, or they might have been Germans trying to insure better treatment; or maybe Burgett just didn't understand what they were trying to say—he got the "nicht schiessen" right, but perhaps that's all.

Some old soldiers may find it hard to believe in the colonel who submitted willingly to the commands of the sergeant in charge of training; the fat doctor in the battalion aid station who was more interested in pistols than his patients; the nurses who said they were all from Detroit; the piggy-back ride on another man's parachute. The thrust of Burgett's perception sweeps away all doubt.

Some pictures will not square exactly with the military life that millions of Americans came to know. But there were many different American "armies" and many different "wars"—assignments ranged from the jungles of the South Pacific to an office in New York City; duties varied from pounding a typewriter to passing the ammunition; there were engineers and truck drivers, machine gunners and cooks, each contributing in his own way and in whatever place he happened to be. Burgett writes of his own war—his own time and place—and though he remains close to his own experience, he speaks for a generation of Americans who, despite a diversity of assignment and a wide disparity of duty, were subjected to the common condition of military service and are still bound together, no matter where they served or what uniform they wore, no matter what dangers they faced or what boredom they supported.

What did the war do to this generation? How did it shape the lives and futures of those who returned and of those who waited? Burgett has unconsciously illuminated these questions in his memoir of Everyman who was seared in the flame of combat.

—Martin Blumenson

1

TRAINING FOR COMBAT

During the winter of 1942, my older brother, Elmer, went into military service. He was well over six feet tall, blond, blue-eyed, broad-shouldered, 180 pounds, and had only a twenty-eight-inch waist. He was not yet twenty. The neighborhood gang got together and gave him a "beer-brawl" send-off from the basement of our home on the west side of Detroit.

Shortly after he had gone, we received a letter from him telling us that he had joined the Paratroops, a little known outfit at that time. He wrote that it took a good man to get in, and an even better one to stay in. This was incentive enough for me, and I could hardly wait until I turned eighteen to prove myself. Knowing that neither Dad nor Mother would sign for me to enter military service before I became of age, I went to my draft board and signed a voluntary induction slip. This way I would be called up on the very next draft after my eighteenth birthday, and my parents would be none the wiser.

I became of age April 5, 1943, and was ordered to re-port to the Induction Center May 3rd. Several men from the different branches of the service were in the main lobby trying to get recruits to join their particular branch of service. The Air Corps and Navy men were busy signing men up, and for a moment I nearly joined the Navy; but then I spotted a paratrooper standing alone next to a small table at the left of the room. He approached several men and asked them to sign up for the Paratroops; but they shied away from him and crossed to the other side of the room. Walking over to him, I said that I would like to join the 'Troops, and he looked at me in shocked disbelief—like a salesman who had just made his first sale.

The recruiter filled out a form to which I signed my full name, Donald Robert Burgett; then he had me sign two papers which stated, "I do hereby volunteer to jump from a plane, while in flight, and land on the ground via para-chute." Then he shook both my hands, patted me on the back, and walked halfway back across the room with me thanking me every step of the way. After a close physical the group I was with was sworn in, given a meal and told to report to the railroad station on May 11th for duty.

My first look at the Fort Benning "Frying Pan" was like looking at heaven; so unlike the barren plains above the rim rock in Kansas, where I had taken my basic. Here were tall green pines; and everywhere in the distance, I could see evidence of swamp and even streams and rivers. The only fly in the ointment was the sand; hardly any grass at all, just sand. The trees reminded me a little of the vast evergreen forests back home in Michigan, but the sand was strictly out of place as far as I was concerned.

Small barracks stood in orderly rows behind a group of weather-beaten tents. The barracks weren't painted, and there was no glass in the windows—just large wooden shutters jutting out over the screened openings, to be let down in case of foul weather. These buildings were set up on short posts or footings; each had two steps up to a door opening set in the center of the front. Some of the dwellings even had doors on the door openings. Two rows of these barracks faced each other, forming a sort of street down the center. At one end, the mess halls ran at right angles with the company street, forming a large "T." At the other end, and set apart from the company street, were the latrines; then farther down the hill, and closer to the blacktop road, was the P.X. and gambling equipment — one-armed bandits and all.

We had disembarked from the trucks and were milling around the mess halls under the pines when one of the best built men I had ever seen, wearing a white T-shirt, jump pants and boots, strode over to us. He had blue eyes set in a handsome tanned face, with shaggy eyebrows and close-cropped hair, both bleached blond by the sun. Walking with an air of authority, he approached us and bellowed at a man with his hands in his pockets, "Gimme twenty-five!"

The man just stood there with a dumbfounded look and asked, "Twenty-five what?"

"Push-ups," came the reply. "What the hell do you think? Make it right now, or you'll get fifty the next time I tell you."

The man dropped into a prone position and started pumping out the required amount. The newcomer then introduced himself as one of the cadre, and a sergeant. Just then he noticed another man leaning against a tree and asked if the prospective trooper thought the tree was going to fall over. The man answered that he was just resting himself. The sergeant told him that no one ever rested around here, and that he could go on holding the tree up until he was told to stop. He then made the man lean forward against the tree and push with all his might, and remain there until he finished talking to us.

The sergeant then briefed us on a few unwritten rules that we had to live by as long as we were in camp. The cadre sergeants were boss, law and order and second only to God in this camp. At no time was a trooper allowed to sit down, lean against anything or stand in a resting attitude when he was outside the confines of his own barracks. Another thing that he wanted to make clear was that at no time was a trooper allowed to walk from one point to another, unless under order to do so; he must run or double-time. When falling out and into formation, a trooper had to run all the way to formation and was allowed only two walking steps to get into ranks. If he took more than two steps it was automatically twenty-five push-ups, the first time; fifty, the next; seventy-five, the third time; and so on. By this time, the man leaning against the tree was quivering all over, and sweat was dripping off his forehead. The sergeant told him to recover, and then, turning to the rest of us, he said, "We're going to be tough on everyone here, and don't expect any sympathy from any of us at any time, because we are going to do everything we can to make you quit the Paratroops."

"Follow me," he ordered. And counting cadence, he marched us to a group of weather-beaten tents.

"This will be your home until you're assigned barracks," he announced.

We stored our gear in tents that were empty; then he marched us around the camp and down the road overlooking the airfield, and briefed us on the different fields and buildings. We were about two miles from the tents when dark clouds rolled up on the horizon and a summer storm threatened to overtake us. Our tent flaps were up, and unless someone were there to close them, everything we owned would get soaked. Rain darkened the runways on the airfield below and came streaking toward us.

"Let's see if we can outrun the rain," the sergeant bellowed. And we started the two-mile run back to tent city in the Frying Pan; we made it, but not quite in time. Lowering the tent flaps didn't help much; a heavy rain on that barren ground, and small rivers were soon running through our floor areas, eroding channels around our bunks and barrack bags.

The next day we were assigned to companies and put into barracks according to alphabetical order. This was the activating of the 541st Parachute Regiment. My barracks, the last one on the street, were close to the latrines; but this was considered an asset, for we didn't have far to travel when we had to go to the toilet or take a shower. We were allowed one day to get squared away on clothing issue: jump suits, boots and special equipment. Then our training began.

Five o'clock the following morning we fell out, stripped to the waist, to begin our first day as paratroopers. Every morning after this, rain or shine, we fell out, wearing only jump boots and pants, naked from the waist up. It was still dark as we answered to roll call, and after everyone was accounted for, we were told that this was the first step in separating the men from the boys. We were then given the order to double-time, and we started running in step to the cadence count of the T-shirted sergeant, down the sandy road of the Frying Pan and onto the black top leading toward the Alabama Ferryboat landing on the Chattahoochee River.

After a mile I began to breathe pretty hard, but knew that my second wind would come soon and the running would seem easier. We all expected the noncom to give quick march pretty soon, but we kept going on and on without any sign of the break we were used to getting in the regular infantry. Our feet beat a steady slapping tattoo on the asphalt, and with the sergeant setting the pace, we moved as a single body over the road through the early hours of the morning. After a few more miles my body seemed to be operating on its own, my legs driving in a steady rhythm, my chest sucking in and letting out deep lungfuls of air, while I retreated, mentally, to an inner corner of my brain to relax in thought and go along for the ride.

Making a wide circuit of the countryside, we were heading back toward the Frying Pan when the man in front of me began to weave back and forth a little; this brought me back to reality. In a little while he began to stagger quite a bit. Suddenly he pitched forward on his face and rolled over on his back. The men behind him spread out and ran by on either side while the sergeant yelled for us to keep going and not pay any attention to him. Two more men fell out long before we reached the center of a field, and the same orders were given—to keep going and leave them alone. Once in the field we were immediately formed into ranks and began calisthenics, starting with side-straddle hops and going the full course to push-ups and other exercises, to cool off after our six-mile run.

Double-timing back to the company area, we fell out for breakfast, after which we were allowed a few minutes to wash up before starting our day's work. Breakfast consisted of cornflakes and a canteen cup of black coffee; half the coffee was used to pour over the cornflakes to make them soft enough to eat. After chow we double-timed down the same road we had taken earlier, but then cut off onto a trail through the woods and across the creek. Jumping from rock to rock across the water and scrambling up the other bank, we re-formed and continued to double-time, until we came out of the woods and onto a road that encircled the Air Force barracks. The Air Force was just falling out for reveille, and our sergeant yelled out extra loud as we ran by, "What did the little dog say when he scraped his ass on the barbed wire?" To which we all replied, as loud as we could, "Ruff, Ruff, Ruff." This went over like a lead balloon with the men who were just waking up, but they didn't offer any protests; evidently they had been through this with troopers who had preceded us. Finally we came to a stop in front of a large hangar and received instructions on what to expect inside and how to act.

An instructor in "A" stage told us that we weren't volunteering for any picnic; that most of us would die in combat. "In fact," he said, "if any man lives through three missions, the government will fly that man home and discharge him. You know as well as I do that Uncle Sam isn't going to discharge anyone during wartime, so now you know what your chances are of living through this war. You haven't got a chance!"

This reminded me of the story where a captain called three men to him and said he was sending them on a patrol behind enemy lines. "The reason we're sending three of you," he said, "is that only one of you will get back; the other two will die." Each one of the soldiers glanced at his buddies, and thought to himself, "Gee, I'm going to miss these guys, and they're such good guys, too."

I didn't give a damn. Some inner force kept telling me that I was going to make it; I was going to survive; I was going to become a paratrooper and live through the war, and nothing in this world was going to stop me.

Here at the packing sheds we were to be given instructions for folding and packing parachutes, and to learn, we would pack our own chutes for our first five jumps. Inside we were assigned, four men each, to long, highly polished tables, where we stood at rigid attention until the instructor commanded, "Stow equipment!" At the first word we took hold of our caps with our right hands; at the second word we slapped the tables hard with them. Then we took off our shirts, folded them neatly and stored them on shelves under the tables. We were then familiarized with the type of chute we would be jumping with—the T-5 assembly, consisting of a twenty-eight foot canopy with as many panels, each panel being made up of four panel sections. The top or center of the canopy, which was known as the apex, contained an eighteen-inch hole to let the surplus air escape and keep the chute from oscillating; it was supposed to, that is. Twenty-eight suspension lines, each twenty-two feet long, ran from the canopy to four cotton-web risers; they were attached, seven each, to the risers by metal rings called connector links. The risers were actually the ends of the harness that were constructed in such a way as to loop around the body, pass through the crotch and back up to the shoulders again. This particular type of chute was designed to open in the prop blast which created an opening shock of approximately five G's.

The unique construction of the harness had a tightening effect around the body much like Chinese finger cuffs, which absorbed the shock, rather than yanking up through the crotch. The harness also had a bellyband that held the smaller reserve chute in front of the wearer, and the wide part that fit the seat was appropriately called "the saddle." A canvas-covered rectangular wire frame on the back, in which the canopy, suspension lines and part of the risers were stored, was called the pack tray. A fifteen-foot static line, attached from a cover on the pack tray to a cable inside the plane, ripped the pack cover off as the trooper jumped free of the ship, pulling the whole works out of the pack tray. The prop blast would then blow the chute open and snap the break cord, tied between the static line and the apex of the canopy. The opening time for this chute was not more than three seconds, which permitted us to make low altitude jumps in mass formation.

The crew at each table was issued several small canvas bags about an inch and a quarter in diameter and about eighteen inches long, which were filled with fine lead shot.

The shot bags were placed across the folded canopies, keeping them from spilling off the tables, while the suspension lines were being stowed in the pack tray. After an hour or so of instruction in the packing of practice chutes, we fell out for more calisthenics.

We were doing push-ups in one of the sawdust pits when the instructor, who was counting cadence from an elevated platform, suddenly asked if we were tired.

"No!" came the chorused answer, for we knew better than to say "Yes."

"O.K.," he replied, "let's keep going."

Noontime we ran back to the company area and had chow that was a little more nourishing than breakfast. The afternoon was a close pattern of the morning training, except that we were shown more about jumping and the equipment that would train us for our first jump. One ingenious device, called the plumber's nightmare, was a network of pipes built about twenty feet high and wide, and about eighty feet long. The men climbed up one end, then across the top and wormed their way back and forth through it in a prearranged course that was said to work to the fullest extent every muscle in the body.

The day ended about five in the afternoon after more running and push-ups. I have never done so many push-ups in my life. Evening chow was nothing to raise any flags over, one helping of unrecognizable hash, black coffee and no bread. We were all tired, and knew that reveille would come early, so we turned in about nine, without anyone bitching about the "lights-out" order yelled down the street by the first sergeant.

Late that night I woke up as someone bumped against

my bunk and staggered across the room making loud noises. Some of the other men woke up too, and we turned on the lights to find that the noisy one was the first man who fell out of the run early that morning. He fell on his bunk and lay face down for a few minutes, then slowly rolling over on his back, he looked at the ceiling, and without talking to anyone in particular, he said, "I tried to keep up. I couldn't help it if I passed out. They let me lay out there all this time. When I came to, I was too weak to crawl, and after lying in the hot sun, I passed out again. I wasn't able to make it in until the sun went down and the air cooled off."

"You mean they didn't send an ambulance for you, or even try to get you to a dispensary?" one of us asked.

"No," he answered. "And if this is the way they treat a man, they can all go to hell and stay there. I'm signing the quit slip." He finally fell asleep with his clothes on, without trying to get under the covers, and refusing any help from any of us.

The next morning we fell out on the double again, and a few of the men got push-ups for taking extra steps while falling into formation. The sergeant called the names of the three men who had fallen out of the run the day before, and told them to report to the orderly room; they were no longer in the Paratroops.

"I told you we were separating the men from the boys," he said, "and we can't use anyone that can't take it." The other two men protested, but it did them no good; they were out, and that was that.

"Where will they be sent?" one of the men asked.

"To the M.P.s!" was the sergeant's reply with a look of disgust. "And I don't want to hear any more about them."

The second day was a copy of the first, except more physical training was added and a little more training on the packing and care of parachutes. The runs lengthened to nine miles every morning before breakfast, and the push-up punishment came more often, even for no reason at all.

One sergeant asked a trooper, "How long is a string?"

The trooper answered, "I don't know."

The sergeant said, "Oh, a dummy, eh. Give me twenty-five."

Then turning to another trooper, he asked the same question, but this trooper answered, "Twice as long as half of it."

The sergeant looked the trooper square in the eye and said, "A smart ass, huh. Give me fifty."

Everything was done on the double; but when any of the instructors wanted something done even faster, they would yell, "Hubba-hubba" one time. We were told this was Yiddish for "Hurry, hurry," but I never took the trouble to find out if this were really true. This came to be just about the most popular saying all through our paratroop career.

Three weeks of "A" stage passed fairly fast; but still, our physical training didn't let up, even when we went into "B" stage, except that we didn't receive quite as much of it. "B" stage was designed to better acquaint us with getting out of the plane, controlling the chute in the air and landing without getting hurt.

One test was the harnesses or "Nut Crackers," as we

called them. Regulation parachute harnesses were hung from hoops that looked like wagon wheels suspended horizontally about fifteen feet above the ground by a steel cable, and were arranged around a rectangular platform. The men would mount the steps to the top of the platform and get into the harness; then, at a command from the sergeant, they would jump off the platform and hang suspended, with feet about three feet off the ground. While hanging in this position, we were taught how to guide a chute by pulling on the risers, and how to assume a body position best suited for landing. We weren't allowed the time to adjust the harness to fit ourselves; so, when we jumped off the platform, the loose straps snapped up into the crotch, earning this device the name "Nut Cracker." Most of the men weren't eager to go through this exercise more than once. Next came the landing trainers, short-jumped platforms and mock-up doors.

By now the men were getting into pretty good condition and were bragging that they could take anything the Army could throw at them. The sergeants let the air out of us by stepping up their bitching, yelling and browbeating. One of them used to look at us while we were doing push-ups in formation and yell that we looked like a bunch of over-worked prostitutes.

"Get the sway out of your backs!" he'd holler.

A few more men had left our ranks; but the rest of us were bound and determined to see this thing through if it killed us. The runs and push-ups were getting easier now; in fact, I didn't even mind the nine-mile runs any more and wasn't at all tired at the end.

The run to the packing shed wound through the woods

and across a small stream with high banks. The voices of the men would ring out through the trees in the crisp, frosty, early morning air as the men put everything they had, from the depths of their lungs, into the song, "I've Got Sixpence." Singing was one of the few privileges allowed us and we took full advantage of it.

After the packing sheds we went to an area that contained several platforms from four to eight feet in height. Every man put on a dummy chute filled with sawdust and went through the act of jumping off the platforms, landing properly and doing a right or left front tumble, or whatever the instructor called for. On a tumble we had to recover at attention—that is, to jump, hit the ground, roll over head first on the shoulder called for, complete the roll across the back, then the buttocks, and come to a standing position, at attention, without taking a step to halt the forward momentum of the body, and remain in that position until ordered, "As you were," or "Recover," by one of the sergeants. We had to jump off one of the eight foot platforms, do a right tumble, run around, get in line and jump again with a left front tumble, then backward, both ways.

Lambart jumped, but instead of recovering after the tumble he lay on the ground groaning.

"What's the matter?" asked the instructor.

"I broke my leg," Lambart told him.

"Baloney, I don't see any bones sticking out. Get up there and jump again."

Lambart jumped again, and this time there was no doubt about it. His leg was broken.

The sergeant looked down at him and said, "Well, now you can ride in the ambulance and take a little time off."

From the first day of "A" stage the noncoms constantly harassed us with a little reflex game called "jab-jab." No matter what we were doing or where we were at, a sergeant would call out "jab" whenever he felt the urge. We were then obliged to double our right fist and hit our left shoulder. A second command of "jab," and we would hit our right shoulder with our left hand and leave our hands in that position until the command "Recover" was given. Then the noncoms would try to trap as many as they could by rapidly yelling "jab, jab; recover; jab." Mixing the command in rapid succession would always confuse someone, and the sergeants would gleefully dole out more push-ups.

Our first test in height came in the mock-up door that was built atop a forty-foot tower; and, although this doesn't sound high, I know of many men who would rather jump from a plane than go off the top of this short jump. A cable ran from the top of the mock-up door and downward on an angle to the ground. A trolley wheel rode on the steel cable and attached to the wheel were two long risers that were fastened to the jumper's parachute harness; this allowed the trooper to jump from the tower and free fall to within a few feet of the ground before being jolted to an abrupt halt, and to slide down the length of the cable until his feet touched the ground. He would then release the risers from his harness, and by a long rope tied to the pulley, tow the apparatus back to the tower where the sergeant at the top could grab it and fasten the next man up for his jump.

We passed through "A" and "B" stages and entered "C" stage. During these different stages we kept up the double-timing, push-ups and the jab-jab game, and took all the harassment the noncoms could throw at us. We even looked forward to the evenings when we could get dressed up and go into Phenix, Alabama, for a night of drinking, fighting with the armored or M.P.s and making out with the local girls, which wasn't hard to do. Most of the time we got back to the barracks with just enough time to grab an hour's sleep before falling out for another day of just plain hard times.

The morning of our first day in "C" stage we again went to the packing sheds and packed chutes for more practice. The last table to finish packing their chutes had to stay and sweep out the entire hangar while the rest of us lounged around outside on a ten-minute break. We were sitting outside in the warm sun—officers and men mixed, for in the jump school rank meant nothing except the sergeants in charge. A sergeant approached a colonel: "You look too comfortable," he said. "Get that broom and sweep the road in front of the hangars until I tell you to stop." The colonel took the rope attached to the broom, looped it over his shoulders and started pulling it up and down in front of the rest of us. The broom was a jerry-built rig of a number of heads of push brooms nailed to a two-by-twelve plank several feet long, and usually required two or three men to pull it by the rope. As the colonel passed us, he glared from under sweat-soaked eyebrows and growled that all the while he was in the ranks years ago, sergeants told him what to do; now that he was a full colonel, they were still telling him what to do. "It'll end some day," he murmured "then watch out."

Just before going up on the 250-foot towers we each had a turn at putting on a parachute, lying on the ground and being blown across the field by an airplane engine prop. After we had skidded on our bellies or backs for a ways, the instructor would order what type of recovery and chute collapse he wanted. The trooper had to get it right or be blown across the ground time after time, until he did get it right. It wasn't unusual to see troopers with great holes worn in the knees and elbows of their fatigues, and sometimes through these holes you could see that patches of skin were also missing. Then troopers put on live parachutes, hooked the opened canopies into large rings or hoops and were hoisted, three at a time, to the top of one of the towers. One at a time they were released, to float to the ground, while an instructor ordered them to slip right, slip left or to make a body turn.

On the next to the last day of "C" stage I was hanging from a yardarm, 250 feet in the air, waiting to be dropped, when I saw in the distance a large caravan of automobiles approaching camp on one of the paved roads. The cars came to a stop between the jump towers and the airfields. I was more interested in them than I was in the chute and had to grab the risers fast when the sergeant turned me loose. On the ground the noncom told me it was a good thing that I didn't foul up; it was President Roosevelt in the convoy, here on inspection tour. I wish I could have seen him closer, but many people have never seen him, even at a distance. I considered myself lucky, for President Roosevelt was one of the greatest men who ever lived.

That night several of us went into town. We were drinking in a small bar, when two troopers began to argue over who would have the honor of buying the next drink. In this case they both wanted to be the one to buy. Finally they got so mad that one challenged the other to a cutting duel. They held left hands, put their left feet together toe to toe and held switchblade knives in their right hands. The bartender took off out the back way, and several civilians left the scene in a hurry too, but most of us stayed, fascinated by the prospect of a fight.

A trooper standing near the bar threw a handkerchief in the air between the two men. They watched it until it hit the floor. Once it touched the floor the two duelists tried to indian wrestle each other into the best position to use their knives. They strained, lost and regained footing and circled, then one of the knives flashed so fast that the actual strike was hardly seen. The second trooper grunted as the blade went between his ribs, but he didn't go down. Instead he countered with a stab that caught the first man in the back above the kidneys. The first trooper dropped to his knees, and at the same time pulled his opponent forward to him and sunk his blade into his ribs, then pulled it forward, opening a long wound in his buddy's left side. The second trooper made a sound like he was trying to vomit and fell to his knees. Just as he went forward on his face, he made one last plunge that caught his friend in the thigh.

The doors burst open and M.P.s came in on the double, followed by the bartender. The M.P.s disarmed the two prone and bleeding troopers, listened to our versions of what had happened and settled down at a table to wait for the ambulance they had called for on their way to the bar. After a short wait, the ambulance arrived and hauled the duelists away, breathing but not too active. We lifted our glasses of beer, drank a toast to the two men and started

back to camp. They were good buddies and would probably wonder what they were fighting about, when and if
they recovered.

The next morning we again went to the packing sheds,
but this time we drew chutes from the bins that were reserved for jumping only. We were to pack our chutes for
our first jump. At my table the four of us tossed coins to
see who would get to pack their chutes first. I lost and
would have to wait until last. Men were hurrying to get
done so they wouldn't have to sweep the floor of the hangar. There were only six tables left packing when the other
three men and I started on my chute. I had finished the
accordion fold with the "H" iron and carefully lifted the
canopy with both hands to place it on the pack tray, when
suddenly the whole thing squirted out of my arms and
spilled onto the floor. "Oh for God's sake," cried Alvarado.
"We can't start all over now; it'll take too long and we'll
have to sweep this whole goddamned hangar out by ourselves." We took the pack tray from the table, placed it on
the floor next to the canopy and scooped the pile of silk
onto it. While Alvarado and Beddel held the slippery bulk
in place, I tied the break cord, and with Barnes standing
on top of the whole mess I completed lacing the pack
cover on. Standing back and viewing our handiwork I felt
little pangs of doubt surge through me, for the lumpy
mess on the floor looked more like a bag of laundry than a
parachute.

"Oh it'll be all right," said Barnes. "If you get all the
lumps out of it, no one will ever notice the difference."

"Yeh, but I will, and if it doesn't work I'll come back
and haunt you guys for the rest of your lives."

"Who cares," retorted Beddel. "At least we won't have to sweep out the hangar."

Then, jumping up and down on it, I managed to get it flattened enough to pass inspection. We finished with just minutes to spare and the two tables still working had the honor of handling the brooms during break period.

We completed our fourth jump on the high towers that afternoon and were told that we would make a night jump about eleven that night, so all passes were canceled. Most of the men were getting excited now, for we knew that school was almost completed and actual jumping would start next week. Upon completing five jumps we would receive our wings and diplomas and be allowed to blouse our pant legs in the tops of our boots at all times. Right now we were only allowed to blouse them in camp or on a practice jump. The running, push-ups and tower jumping were second nature to us now, and we were looking forward to the real thing, the wet run.

Night came on and we found ourselves assembled at the foot of the towers, waiting our turn. A sergeant was calling names from a roster and checking them off when the jump was completed. First, they explained that there would be a man with a flashlight on the ground a short distance from the tower. He would give a quick flash of light toward the trooper at the top of the tower, then turn it off. The trooper would then have to guide his chute toward the point where he last saw the light in order to keep the wind from blowing him into the steel girders. The night was so black that a man at the top of the tower couldn't see the ground, and swinging from the single cable, it was almost impossible to tell which direction the wind was coming from. Three men at a time were hauled aloft on different arms and left to hang there, 250 feet in the air, until the instructors were ready to release them. The big noncom yelled up through the night air, "Do you see your beam, number one?"

"No," came the disturbed answer as the jumper looked frantically for the sliver of light.

"Release number one," the sergeant bawled.

"Wait," came the voice through the darkness from atop the tower, but he was already on his way down, clawing at his risers in hopes that he was guiding the chute in the right direction. Again came the question, "Do you see your beam, number three?"

"Nooo-o."

"Release number three." This went on, with very few of the men actually ever seeing the beam. Only one man piled into the steel structure and hung there until the instructors could climb up and get him down.

"Boy, you have to hubba-hubba one time to home in on that beam," I said.

"You're not just woofing there," said Beddel. "They just turn you loose and hope for the best. Maybe the sergeants want to get home early tonight."

We finally finished, with two jumps each, and headed back to the barracks for a few hours' sleep. We got Sunday off, and most of us stayed in camp, playing poker or craps or taking turns at the slot machines.

On Monday morning we drew our chutes, put them on and waited in the sweat sheds for our turn to load on the planes for our first jump. Our first one was to be at 1200 feet, the second one at 1000, the third and fourth at 800, the fifth, a night jump, at 1000. Once qualified as troopers, we would receive an extra fifty dollars a month, regardless of the amount of jumps we would make per month. But we would be required to make a minimum of one jump every three months. The day seemed hotter than ever before, and sweat trickled from under my armpits and ran down my elbows, while a weak feeling came into the pit of my stomach. This is what they call "butterflies in the belly," I guessed.

Up until recently our first sergeant had been a Jew named Abraham Axelrod, one of the best men I have ever known; there wasn't anything he wouldn't do for us men. I think it was for this reason that he was relieved of his rank and another sergeant took his place. There was nothing personal in our dislike for the new first sergeant, it was just that we felt that we were cheated of a good thing and didn't like the bum deal that Axelrod got.

When our stick finally moved outside to the runway and a sergeant came down the ranks checking our harness, static lines and break cords, he stopped for some time in front of the new first sergeant, looked hard at him and asked, "Don't your men like you?"

"I don't care what they don't like," he answered. "Why?"

"Because someone wrapped bailing wire from your static line to your canopy instead of silk for a break cord; you had better draw another chute from the packing bins."

The first sergeant's face turned a dark red as he turned

to scowl at us; then, stamping back to the hangar he grumbled, "Someone here really doesn't like me, but I'll put a finish to that." He returned just in time to load on the C-47 with us and took his seat without saying a word.

This was the first time I had ever been in a plane in my life, and I couldn't help feeling the little nerves and muscles twitch and jump in my body as the plane rumbled across the field and into position at the end of a runway. The pilot pushed the throttles forward, and the plane gathered speed and started eating up runway at a fast rate. Looking out the port, I was surprised to see the field, trees and buildings far below and getting smaller. I didn't even know when we had left the ground and become airborne. We started singing the Troopers' song, "Blood Upon the Risers." The words were written to the tune of "The Battle Hymn of the Republic."

"Is everybody happy?" cried the Sergeant, looking
　　up.
Our hero feebly answered "yes," and then they
　　stood him up.
He leaped right out into the blast, his static line
　　unhooked.
He ain't gonna jump no more.
　　　　　　　　　(chorus)

He counted long, he counted loud, he waited for
　　the shock;
He felt the wind, he felt the clouds, he felt the
　　awful drop;

He jerked his cord, the silk spilled out and
    wrapped around his legs.
He ain't gonna jump no more.
           (chorus)

The risers wrapped around his neck, connectors
    cracked his dome;
The lines were snarled and tied in knots, around
    his skinny bones;
The canopy became his shroud, he hurtled to the
    ground.
He ain't gonna jump no more.
           (chorus)

The days he'd lived and loved and laughed kept
    running through his mind;
He thought about the girl back home, the one he'd
    left behind;
He thought about the medics and wondered what
    they'd find.
He ain't gonna jump no more.
           (chorus)

The ambulance was on the spot, the jeeps were
    running wild;
The medics jumped and screamed with glee, they
    rolled their sleeves and smiled;
For it had been a week or more since last a chute
    had failed.
He ain't gonna jump no more.
           (chorus)

He hit the ground, the sound was *splat,* his blood
    went spurting high;
His comrades then were heard to say, "A helluva
    way to die";
He lay there rolling 'round in the welter of his
    gore.
He ain't gonna jump no more.
              (chorus)

There was blood upon the risers, there were brains
    upon the chute;
Intestines were a-dangling from this paratrooper's
    boots;
They picked him up, still in his chute and poured
    him from his boots.
He ain't gonna jump no more.
              (chorus)

CHORUS
Gory, Gory, What a Helluva way to die
Gory, Gory, What a Helluva way to die
Gory, Gory, What a Helluva way to die
He ain't gonna jump no more.

By the time we had finished singing we had made the
run over the Chattahoochee River and were now heading
back across the D.Z. (drop zone). The jump master, wearing a free type chute and standing in the doorway, turned
to us and gave the order, "Stand up and hook up."

"This is it," I thought, "the moment we've been waiting
for." Days of the infantry basic flashed across my mind

along with the thoughts of the struggle to get here and become a paratrooper.

"Check equipment," was our next order. We went through the formality of checking our own gear and the equipment of the man ahead of us. I was scared, but I couldn't quit now; I wouldn't be able to face my buddies, and what about the folks back home?

"Sound off," and the last man in the stick, nearest the cockpit, yelled, "Twelve O.K.," and slapped the man ahead of him on the back. He in turn called out, "Eleven O.K.," then came ten O.K., then nine and so on, down the line to the first man in the stick, standing near the open doorway. The jump master barked, "Stand in the door, close it up tight." The first man pivoted into the doorway, placed his hands on either side of the opening and extended his left foot forward. The next man put his right foot against the first trooper's right foot and his left in behind the lead man. This way he would be ready to pivot to his right into the door as soon as the first man jumped and be ready to go as soon as the jump master tapped his leg. Receiving the signal, he would leap out of the door, turning left toward the tail of the plane at the same time. Now the jump master was kneeling by the lower right side of the door, looking at the ground.

"Is everybody happy?" he yelled.

"Yeh," we all yelled back in chorus. He tapped the first man on the calf of his right leg, and the man shot through the opening like a bullet. His static line snapped taut and vibrated, like a hangman's rope on the gallows. The next man did a quick right pivot and snapped into the doorway; another tap on the leg, a whispered command "Go," and he too disappeared from sight. The men in the stick were moving forward keeping their left foot forward, the right one behind, like a boxer—never crossing the two. The next man went out, then the next; the door was coming closer and closer. I could hear the wind whistling by the opening and see the static lines stretched tight between the steel anchor cable and the edge of the door. It was just a matter of seconds since the first man went out, and we were still shuffling forward toward the door.

"What the hell am I doing here, I ought to have my head examined." The man in front of me turned into the doorway and I automatically took up position of second man. My mouth went dry and I felt a shiver go through me as the wind from outside hit my sweat-soaked fatigues.

"There's still time to quit, sign the quit slip and go to the M.P.s," I thought; but the man in front of me was gone, and I found myself standing in the opening. All the ground instructor's words came to me very clear now, "Keep your fingers outside the door, don't look down, watch the horizon." A slight tap on the right leg and my body unleashed like a steel spring, straight out into nothing.

I don t remember hearing the command "Go," but now I was alone in the air. Everything seemed to be moving in slow motion; there was no sensation of falling, not even like that of an elevator ride. The tail of the plane moved toward the right, while the ground came up on the left and swung slowly around to the front. I yelled out at the top of my voice, "One thousand," and heard the canopy crackling over my head as the prop blast caught it.

"Two thousand." The connector links whistled past, and

I ducked my head a little farther and cradled my reserve in my left arm, ready to throw the canopy out, if and when I pulled the rip cord with my right hand. Now the ground was directly in front of me again, "Three thous—," the opening shock nearly sent me through the bottoms of my own boots, and I could feel my cheeks pull out away from my teeth. Less than three seconds had elapsed from the time I had left the plane till the opening shock. It was quite an experience to be traveling forward with the momentum of the plane at better than a hundred miles an hour, then being blasted backward at the same rate of speed by the prop blast. The ground in front of me stopped its upward swing and started settling slowly back underneath. This was crazy, the feeling of being suspended in mid-air, while everything else moved around me. Actually I had tumbled over and over until the chute opened, then started a normal descent with a slight oscillation. I opened the risers and looked up; the canopy checked out—no blown panels, Mae Wests or broken or snarled lines. None of the other chutes around me looked as if they were going up or down, which meant that my fall was at a normal rate of speed and there was nothing to worry about. Checking my wind drift by watching my feet in relation to the movement of the ground, I turned my back into the wind by crossing the risers behind my neck and pulling gently outward on them until I was in the right position. A jeep and ambulance were converging under me as the sergeant in the jeep called up through a megaphone, "Number eight, you're bicycling; stop your bicycling." Unconsciously I was reaching for the ground, first with one foot, then the other. I looked at the horizon, took up what I thought to be a good body position and hit the ground.

Pain shot through my whole body sending bright flashes across my eyes, almost blacking me out. Rolling over face down, collapsing the chute and getting out of the harness was just about more than I could bear. Every time I tried to stand, the pain shot through my leg with such fierceness that I would fall down and almost pass out. I didn't want to show weakness by calling for help. Pulling my jump knife, I cut the laces of my boot, then crawled to the canopy, rolled it up and fastened it to the pack tray with the belly band. The trucks that were to take us back to the packing sheds were clear across the other side of the field. Cactus Hill lay between me and them, so I started crawling or pulling myself along on my belly through the spines and thistles toward them. Suddenly, the jeep I had seen from the air came racing toward me. "Oh boy, help," I thought; but as the sergeant pulled up beside me he leaned over and asked, "Where's your chute, trooper?"

"Back there," I said, pointing to the package on the ground.

"Get it and bring it with you to the packing sheds," he commanded.

After eating me out for bicycling on the way down, he told me that I would have to find my own way back; the ambulance was reserved for legitimate breaks. Then he drove off, the wheels of the jeep kicking dust in my face.

"That's a hell of a thing to do," I thought, as I crawled back and retrieved the chute. The only way I could travel was to lie on my side, throw the chute forward, crawl to it and repeat the procedure over and over again. Finally another jeep came up and this time a sergeant leaned over the steering wheel and said, "That's the spirit we like around here"; then he drove off. I crawled for what seemed to be hours and finally came in view of the trucks, but was still out of hearing range when the last one drove off; all my yelling and waving did no good, no one saw me.

"Oh my GI aching airborne back," I thought. If I knew how to cry, I believe that I could have done it then.

It was getting dark and spending the night out here certainly didn't appeal to me at all. With a torn jump suit, a skin full of thorns and a battered parachute I finally made it to a black top road and managed to flag a car down. The driver, a civilian P.X. worker, was kind enough to drive me to a dispensary where the medics X-rayed the leg and told me that it had only a small fracture and torn ligaments. They put a cast on it and told me to return to my barracks.

"Can I have a pair of crutches?" I asked.

"We don't have any, too many other troopers with breaks worse than yours have got them," replied the medic.

Hobbling outside, I cut a branch from a tree to use as a crutch and hitched a ride with a jeep driver to my barracks; he said he was going my way anyhow. All my buddies looked at me and asked, "What happened to you, take a furlough or something?"

"Hell no, I broke my leg; I suppose I'm too late for chow too."

"Yeh," Alvarado said. "But you can have my candy bar. I don't want it anyway." He handed me the chocolate bar that he had already partially unwrapped for himself. I thanked him and said that it would probably save my life.

The following morning we fell out for reveille and the first sergeant was still mad because someone had tried to kill him by tying his break cord with wire. He invited anyone who didn't like him to take one step forward. Three husky troopers did, and the top kick called us to attention and marched us down behind the latrines. I followed behind, hopping along with the crude crutch. Behind the latrine the sergeant told the men to strip to the waist and he did the same, so there would be no rank showing. He took all three on at one time, and though he was a spindly-looking man, we soon saw that he was nothing but bone, muscle and lightning-fast fists. The sergeant weaved and lashed out with arms that looked as if they were laced with piano wire. This man was a real scrapper. Within minutes two of the troopers were face down and the third was on his knees, unable to stand. The first sergeant looked around and announced, "I'm still the first sergeant here and anytime anyone wants to challenge my authority, we can settle it behind the latrines, with no rank showing." A challenge to a noncom, with no rank showing, was not uncommon in the Paratroops and no court martial ever came of it regardless of who won. After the fight behind the latrines, the men had great respect for the sergeant and no one tried to wire his break cord any more.

Each day I lay in my bunk watching the men go out in the morning for their physical training and again in the afternoon to make another jump. The fourth day arrived and my buddies told me they would be making one jump in the morning and another late that night, around midnight. The sun shone brightly and there was very little wind, a perfect day for jumping; the up-drafts should make for some soft landings. The men were jubilant when they came in for noon chow and could hardly wait for nighttime to complete their school. The morning jump had gone well. I felt sick inside about missing the graduation exercises and being left behind by the men I had gone through so much with. Men bought whiskey and beer and stashed the bottles away for the celebration that would come after the last qualifying jump. Just at dusk they fell out, and I wished each one luck as they filed past me and went out the door. In turn they encouraged me and said it wouldn't be too long before I would rejoin the outfit. Lying on the bunk, I could hear them singing "I've Got Sixpence" at the top of their voices as they double-timed out of the Frying Pan and down the road leading to the airfield. Their voices rang in the cool night air.

I nursed a bottle of beer one of the troopers had given me before they left the barracks. I envied them. Time dragged and finally I dozed off. I don't know how long I had been asleep, but the first thing I was aware of was the whooping and hollering of a lot of men in the direction of the mess halls. They swung down the company street, swaggering, singing and giving out yells of victory. They were paratroopers now. The long weeks of "A," "B," "C" and "D" stages were over, along with the exercises, humiliations and punishments. Lights were coming on in all the barracks; bottles were opened and men were singing, making toasts and telling each other of their own personal experiences on different jumps. I kept waiting, but none of my buddies showed up in the barracks. "Maybe they've stopped in the next hut," I thought, "to celebrate a little with the others before coming home." After a while I could wait no longer and taking my crutches—I had managed to get a pair by this time—hobbled next door. All the troopers welcomed me in and offered me drinks from bottles and told me to help myself to the beer.

"Where are Alvarado, Barnes, Beddel and the rest of my bunch?" I asked.

"Hell, didn't you know? They're all dead."

"Dead? But how?" I asked.

"The plane took up jumping attitude, and as the pilot throttled back on the port engine, the starboard conked out; at that altitude they didn't stand a chance. The ship hit the ground and exploded; everyone was burned to death." We toasted their departure, "Here's to the last one; here's to the next one. Here's to the ones we left behind." We lived it up that night, celebrating like there would be no tomorrow. Things finally died down and men started hitting the sack. I went back to my hut, and not bothering to turn on the lights, went to bed. Just before dozing off, I thought, "If it hadn't been for my leg, I would have been on that plane." Twenty-four men, the jump master and crew, all dead.

A few days later the outfit pulled out and headed for Camp Mackall, leaving me behind to make up my qualifying jumps and catch up later. Later that day a new bunch arrived at the Frying Pan, looking about wonderingly, and memories of our first arrival and the faces of the men now dead clouded my mind. Later that day a noncom told me

to report to a barrack section of camp overlooking the airfield where other troopers, like myself, were healing from
minor injuries and waiting to finish their required jumps to
graduate. After reporting to the orderly room I was assigned a barracks and told to make myself at home. Things
here were very lax, quite a contrast to what we had been
used to in the Frying Pan. Troopers lounged around in
assorted uniforms, some with casts or bandages on, or
some just hobbling around, almost recovered from whatever trouble they had. The barracks were the large two-
story type and very neat, orderly and comfortable. I
stopped at a day room on my way to my assigned barracks
and saw that it was well furnished; there were pool tables,
jukeboxes and other entertainment facilities. On one wall
hung the paratroopers prayer, in a simple wooden frame.
It went as follows:

The Paratrooper's Prayer

Our Almighty Father, who dwelleth in Washington,
immersed in service records, requisitions, T.S. slips,
red tape and other impedimenta which surroundeth
the Army both in times of peace and in times of war,
hallowed be thy name.

Give us this day our partial pay, and forgive us of
our company bills. Guide us on the path of righ-
teousness by thy all-knowing Articles of War and
Rules and Regulations. Approve our passes and fur-
loughs, for thou knowest ours is not an easy lot to
bear without leisure time.

Deliver us from the hands of non-jumping Military Police, for thou knowest our burdens are manifold. Yea even though by divers devices art these yellow livered Sons of Satan's Concubines, these gutless washouts from thy parachute school, after having thrice been beaten about the head with a shot bag, allowed to don the hated white cap and belt of the Ersatz Gestapo, they falsely cry that they are thy chosen children. We cannot contain ourselves in their presence and assault and mayhem shall abound.

Guide our pleasure-bent footsteps from the lower regions of sin and iniquity known locally as Phenix City, lest we should go astray and contact social uncleanliness which thou so forcefully describeth in thy sex hygiene training film.

Unhook not our static lines, nor yet blow panels in our canopies. Cut not our break cords, and drift us clear of Cactus Hill. Strike with relentlessly swift and horrible death the company clerk who red lineth our payroll and the mess sergeant who robbeth our empty bellies. By the ghosts of those who have preceded us to the Frying Pan and the Alabama area, we pray thee . . . Amen.

In ten days' time my leg was feeling better. The cast was off and although I walked with a limp, I felt it wouldn't be long before I would be ready to jump again. It wasn't. When two close buddies of mine shipped out several days later, I again felt alone and decided to start jumping again. Neither the doctor nor the company commander thought I was ready yet, but I insisted. That afternoon I again found myself double-timing to the packing sheds to pack my

chute. Running was painful and I had to favor my right leg
quite a bit, but once I committed myself to training again I
wouldn't back out.

The next day found us lined up on the wooden benches,
outside the sweat sheds watching other troopers make
their jumps and waiting our turn. Looking through the
glare of a sunny Georgia day, we watched a plane swing
along the Chattahoochee River and come in over the drop
zone at about 1000 feet. The tiny figures tumbled out in
rapid succession and all seemed well until two of the
chutes bumped together in mid-air, and the men became
entangled in suspension lines. One chute collapsed but the
other one held, and for a moment it looked as if they
would still make it O.K.

Jeeps were tearing across the field while a white-shirted
instructor called orders to the men with a megaphone from
one of them. At the same time an ambulance was racing to
the spot on the ground where the two troopers would land.
We talked to the men under our breaths, hoping they
would make it the several hundred feet to the ground
safely. But the man hanging lower than the other pulled
his reserve chute. This is something we were specifically
instructed not to do. The only time a reserve chute is any
good is when the main doesn't open at all or has a serious
malfunction. When two men are entangled, the reserve
can billow up and collapse the main chutes. When a man is
alone (not entangled with another) and his main is open
and he opens his reserve, the reserve being shorter will
blossom next to the shroud lines and just under the canopy
of the main chute. This position holds both canopies on a
sharp angle, allowing the air to spill out of them at a rapid

pace, at times almost doubling the rate of descent. Now, as we watched, the smaller chute unfurled into the main canopy of the top man, collapsing it. The chutes looked like bedsheets fluttering behind the figures as they plummeted earthward. Neither one of the men yelled or made a sound; they must have been too busy trying to untangle the snarled lines and fighting for their lives to know how close they were. The whole mess took place in a matter of seconds as, from front row seats, we saw the men fall to their deaths.

They bounced a couple of feet in the air. I couldn't get over the fact that they bounced; somehow it never occurred to me that a human body would do that. One of the sergeants leaped from a jeep and worked over the bodies a few minutes, then got back in and drove up to us. Climbing out of the jeep he held two pairs of bloodied jump boots from those two men out there.

"Now does anyone want to quit," he said, then handed the boots to the first man in our stick and told him to pass them down from man to man. The boots came to me and I looked close at them. They were bloodied, and a small sliver of white bone protruded through one of them and the blood hadn't congealed yet. After every man in the stick had handled them, the sergeant took the boots back and insisted that surely someone wanted to quit; no one stepped out of line.

A C-47 taxied in front of the hangers, and my stick, along with another, boarded it; within minutes we were airborne, and making the same run that the fateful one had taken a little earlier. The Chattahoochee River lay below

and to right of our flight line. Making a left bank we lev-
eled over the field, and the jump master went through the
rehearsed commands. As lead man in the second stick I sat
across from the door watching as the first stick went out.
We circled the field; then, a couple of sharp commands
from the jump master and I found myself standing in the
doorway. The wind whipped at my cheeks, tugging them
far out from my face. The sergeant knelt at the right side
of the door peeking out at the ground. At the same time
the same inner voice as before went step by step through
the chain of instructions that should make a successful
jump. The jump master looked up and simply said "Go."
Again I leaped into the prop blast and started the count,
"One thousand, two thousand," and again the whole world
swirled around as I tumbled over and over in the air. The
opening shock came and nearly jarred my teeth from my
mouth. But descent was easy and the chute, stretched
tight, shone brightly in the sun. It sure did look good over
my head. Nearing the ground I checked my drift, turned
my back into the wind and made a perfect parade-ground
landing. What a feeling! My leg hurt a little, but the feeling
of being safe and sound made me so jubilant that I patted
my chute and the ground at the same time, while still on
my hands and knees. To think I had actually made a jump
and didn't have any broken bones or other damages! Rolling my chute up and slinging it over my shoulder, I strode
across the field with the other troopers to the waiting
trucks and climbed aboard for the ride back to the packing
sheds. Once in the packing sheds we repacked our chutes
and put them in bins for our jump the next day. The after-

noon was spent in calisthenics and more double timing to keep us in condition.

My first jump had been on October 18, 1943, the second on November 2, 1943 and now the third about eleven o'clock the following morning. We ran to the airfield, put on our chutes and waited our turn to make the drop, every jump putting us closer to getting our wings and rejoining our outfits. The air was crisp and clear at first, but as we waited outside the sweat sheds the air became steadily warmer, and now rivulets of sweat ran down my body. Finally our turn came. We put our clear plastic football-type helmets on and double-timed to the waiting plane. The metal bucket seats were warm and none too comfortable as we strapped the safety belts across our laps. The air was thick and stuffy inside the plane and I could hardly wait for us to start so the wind flow past the open door would clear the air. Looking forward, I could see the pilots in the cockpit; they were wearing sun glasses, shoes and shorts, no shirts, and they had the little windows on either side of the cockpit open to let the cooler air in.

The engines revved up and we moved in a zig-zag pattern to the end of the runway, then with both engines opened all the way, we went down the runway and into the air. The plane jounced a little, like a car traveling over a country road. We followed the same general pattern as before and stood up and hooked up as we swung away from the river, ready for the jump. The whole stick was straining forward toward the door while the first couple of men held them in check, bracing their feet on the floor. I was about halfway back in the stick and could think of nothing else but to get out of the ship and get the damned jump over with. I was thinking of a hot shower and a cold bottle of beer that evening and hoping the canopy would open so I would live to enjoy them. The jump master yelled, "Let's go," and the stick shot forward. Getting to the door I could see that there wasn't enough time to make the pivot or turn, so I just dove head first on an angle out the door and hoped for the best.

The tail of the plane passed overhead and I could hear the crackling of the canopy as it unfurled in the prop blast. The opening shock came and I was floating earthward in bright sunlight, looking at the clear patchwork ground below. I felt as if I had just conquered the world, and my chest swelled as though I were master of gravity itself. Suddenly a trooper yelled for me to get the hell out of the way. Looking around I saw a man coming down on top of me fast. Yanking the left risers, my chute slid off to one side and the other man glided past, close enough for our chute skirts to touch each other. The other chutes in the air were at the same level as myself and falling at the same rate of speed, so I knew that my descent was all right and that the other man must be falling too fast. Looking down I yelled for him to pull his reserve, but he yelled back for me to mind my own damned business.

The ground was close enough now so that I could no longer watch him. I had to pick out a spot to land in. The landing and right-front tumble was in parade-ground fashion, but the wind was a little high. The canopy billowed up and took me belly down through the cactus. Putting the bottom lines together and pulling them in hand over hand I finally managed to collapse the parachute, but not until I had dragged a path clear over Cactus Hill through cactus, briars and rocks. A few more jumps like this and I would have Cactus Hill pretty well cleaned off. The holes in my new jump suit sure did bother me, but not half as much as the ones in my skin. It would be days before I would be able to get all the stickers and thorns out. The next day we packed two chutes but made no jumps. Instead we took a trip by truck across the Chattahoochee River to L and M fields on the Alabama side to look the area over where our night jump would be made. The rest of the day was spent in exercises.

November 5th, about three in the afternoon, we made our scheduled drop with everything coming off according to the book. This was a snap. It hadn't rained for several days now and the sun was shining bright as ever. But this could be hard too, as I soon found out. The up-drafts caused by the sun's heat on the fields filled the chutes, causing them to oscillate more than average. Swinging like the pendulum of a clock, my feet just missed the ground on the way down. The canopy hit first, collapsed, and I was slammed, whip-like, against the ground. I hit one side of a small jeep trail so hard that bright lights flashed in front of my eyes. When I could see clearly again I found that I was lying on the opposite side of the trail with a four-inch split up the back of my helmet and a terrific pain in my right leg. I rolled over on my back and was undoing my harness when another trooper came down on top of me. Covering my head with my arms, I rolled to get out of his way, but his feet caught me in the side and mashed my ribs a little. The trooper scrambled to his feet and still in his harness ran over and asked if I was hurt.

"No," I replied. "But from the bottom you've got the biggest feet I've ever seen."

He apologized for landing on me, then taking his chute headed in the direction of the trucks. Limping along behind I heard someone yell, "Look out"; almost overhead a man came hurtling down with an unopened chute. It was pulled out of the pack tray, but remained closed, a streamer.

The man hit a few yards away, making a sound like a large mattress going "floomp" against the ground, and for the second time in a week I witnessed a man hitting the ground so hard that he actually bounced. Limping over, I looked down at him and nearly fell over when he opened his eyes and asked me, "What happened?"

"Your chute didn't open," I told him.

"You're kidding," he said. "Help me up, I've got to get going."

"You're not going anywhere," a sergeant said as a jeep pulled up, "except to a hospital." The man on the ground protested, saying that he had to make another jump that night.

When he tried to get up all he could do was raise his head a little, then fall back to the ground. It was then I noticed the crosses on his collar; who else but a chaplain could fall 1000 feet with an unopened chute and live? He had suffered a broken leg and internal injuries, but just how bad I never did find out. The noncom told him to lie still until the meat wagon came; the medics would take care of everything from here on out.

"I've told you men a thousand times to check your canopy first when you leave the plane; let this be a lesson to you."

That night I was in the last lift to make the drop and ended up in a planeload of officers. They had put one officer in each stick that night but still two sticks of them were left over at the end of the jumping. The officers looked at me as though I were an intruder in their private club and made me get in the middle of the stick as though I couldn't find my own way to the door.

It was dark inside the plane as well as outside and we could see a long tongue of flame from the exhaust sliding along the outside of the ship. I had never noticed this in the daytime, but evidently it was there all the time; it just showed up better at night. We got the order to stand up and hook up and one of the officers must have expelled some gas, for the smell was pretty bad in the close quarters of the ship. I took advantage of this to get back at them and said, "One of you officers must have crapped your pants; that's a hell of a way for a leader to act." Some of them shuffled around in the dark as if trying to see my face, but just then we got the green light and went out the door. This was my easiest jump; I could hear other chutes popping open in the dark night air but could not see anyone or the ground.

Hitting the ground came as sort of a surprise, for I didn't expect it so soon; we must have jumped a little lower this time. Standing up, still in my harness, I let out a yell that could be heard clear to the Frying Pan. I had made it. I was a trooper now, a full-fledged paratrooper, and would get my wings. No matter what happened they couldn't take that away from me.

2

WAITING FOR COMBAT

THE ELEVENTH DAY WE CAME IN THE SIGHT OF land, and the crew told us it was Ireland. I could see why they call it the Emerald Isle; it was the greenest land I have ever seen. The Empire Anvil docked that night and the following morning we made ready to disembark. People lined the docks and gave the thumbs up sign and the "V" for victory sign with their fingers. Some of them waved, laughed and asked where we were from. This was Belfast, Ireland, a friendly city with some strange sights for a newcomer. Some of the troopers were throwing packs of cigarettes to the dock and the Irish laborers were scooping them up as fast as they hit. We were sure we would always be able to get all we wanted, but soon found out that everything was rationed here—everything.

We disembarked shortly before noon and traveled all afternoon by truck through the Irish countryside, finally arriving at Camp Clandibouy after dark. We were assigned bunks in Quonset huts and marched to a mess hall where we got our first decent meal since Newport News, Virginia, our port of embarkation.

After breakfast the next day we explored the area. A stone tower on a hill overlooked the camp while smaller cottages surrounded it. Men were working in the fields, and we asked them where we were at. They told us this was the Clandibouy estate, that Lord Clandibouy was away at war and that he had rented the U.S. government the land for the camp. They also gave us directions to town, but the gates of camp were guarded and we had orders not to leave camp.

Six of us returned to our barracks, changed from jump suits to class A's, shined our boots and started to look for a way out of camp and into town. One of the men reported that he had been to the other end of camp and that we could get out the back way by going through the obstacle course. The cadre thought no one would be foolish enough to try to go through the course all dressed up and hadn't posted a guard there. We took off on the double, our long overcoats flapping about the calves of our legs as we ran through the woods and onto the obstacle course. After the training we had had, this was a snap. We went over the walls, then ran the length of the elevated planks that ran in a zig-zag pattern over the marshy area and led to a creek. The creek was too wide to jump, but at one point there was a large double "A" frame built over it with ropes hanging from the crossbar. This was the part of the course where the troops had to take a running jump, catch hold of a rope and swing to dry land on the other side.

"Let's go," I said to my buddies, and trotted back a few yards to get a running start. The damned long overcoat kept wrapping around my legs and getting in the way, but it was too late to stop now. At the edge of the water I leaped out, grabbed one of the ropes and swung out over the water. The momentum carried me clear across to the other side and I dropped safely to dry ground. One by one the other men followed until our little buddy from Tennessee was standing alone on the other side. We stood in a group watching as he came loping across the field with coattail flapping. He leaped out, grabbed a rope and made a good swing, but as he reached our side he didn't let go. He swung back and still he didn't let go.

"I don't think I can do it," he said, and by this time we all knew he couldn't for the rope had lost its momentum and now he hung in the middle, right over the water. There was nothing any of us could do, for there were no other poles or ropes that we could hand or throw him. He begged and pleaded with us to do something as his grip loosened and he inched toward the cold water. The closer he got the more he would pull his feet up until finally he looked like a little ball hanging on the end of the rope. By this time most of us were laughing so hard that some of the men were lying on the ground holding their sides, tears streaming from their eyes. One instant he was hanging there in a little ball, glaring at us, the next instant there was a splash and he was standing in water up to his armpits and swearing for all he was worth. I laughed so hard that my sides hurt and could hardly catch my breath as he came wading out on our side of the creek and said, "Well, let's get started, the girls aren't going to wait forever."

The six of us walked down a lane, past a church and into town; all the while Tennessee's boots kept making a squishy sound and he kept mumbling something to himself about the fact that we could have saved him if we had really wanted to. The town didn't look too promising, but as we made a circuit, noting the locations of pubs and the young girls, we heard people talking of a dance that was to take place that night. Herman asked one of the girls where the dance was going to be, and she told him and asked us if we would come to it. We promised we would and thanked her for her hospitality, then headed for the nearest pub. It didn't look like much from the outside, but from the inside it was a different story. There were civilians and GIs all drinking and having a ball. At the moment they were singing "Roll Me Over in the Clover," to the accompaniment of an old piano in the corner. We joined right in, and at first people shunned us because of the scalp locks some of us had gotten just before we were shipped out. But we put our caps on, minded our own manners and soon each of us had a girl sitting on our laps as we drank beer from pint mugs.

Later, taking the girls in tow, we made the rounds of most of the local pubs, then headed unsteadily for the community dance that was by this time in full swing. The townspeople admitted us with a warm welcome and begged us to join the dancing. I didn't know the first thing about dancing, but it looked simple, so I joined with the rest of my buddies. First everyone got in a big circle and then all started singing, "Put your right foot in, put your right foot out," and all the time they were singing they actually put their foot in and out of the circle. With all of this foot and body swinging the beer finally took its toll, and I had to go outside and lay on the nice cool ground.

Herman must have missed me, for the next thing I knew he was shaking me and telling me to come back inside, the dance was breaking up and we had to escort the girls back home. We walked to the square in a group but then split up, for the girls lived in different parts of town.

As we received no training in Camp Clandibouy, most of our days and nights were spent in town. The only thing wrong with this was that while we were gone the men who remained in camp used our bunks for firewood. This left us with nothing to sleep on except our two blankets and the cement floor. I finally managed to swipe a bunk from another barrack, but this one only had two planks and it was like trying to sleep on the top edge of a fence.

After about a week, we started receiving shots and further medical checkups, and it looked as though we were getting ready to ship out again. The rest of the processing was over in a few days, and again we found ourselves under way. This time by truck, train and ferryboat we went from Ireland to Scotland, and then on to England. After several layovers at various camps, we finally ended up in a repel depot from where we were shipped out in small groups at different times to different places. My group arrived by truck at a small town called Aldbourne. A sergeant took us up a small hill and through a gate in a brick wall. "This," he told us, "used to be the stables for a mansion." He said that after duty hours we would have a standing class "A" pass at the orderly room to go into Swindon, a larger town several miles away, and that no pass was needed to roam around Aldbourne.

The stables, or barracks now, were built of wood and

ran the full length of the courtyard with four stalls protruding out at right angles from the main line at four-stall intervals. This gave it the appearance of a large multiple "E" laid out top to bottom or end to end on the ground, however you would look at it. There were four stables to each section with four men to each stable. Each stable also had a Dutch-type door in front with a small window on either side of it. The inside had cobblestone floor, a double bunk on either side and a small stove in the center of the back wall. They were the best barracks I had ever been in, small, neat, comfortable and yet large enough for four men to live in and have a certain amount of privacy, something almost unknown in the service.

Phillips, Benson and myself were assigned to stable 13. As we entered we saw a lone trooper poking up a fire in the stove. When we introduced ourselves he straightened up, looked at each one of us and walked out. Phillips said that like it or not, we would all have to live together. When the trooper returned he told us his name was Liddle. He was well built, had a large jaw and curly hair. He fooled around with his gear while we chose bunks and squared our own gear away. Then without looking up he said, "You'll find the haystack on the other side of the latrines if you want to fill your mattress covers." We thanked him, and with Phillips in the lead we made our way across the courtyard to the haystack and filled the mattress covers as full as we could get them, for we knew that after sleeping on them a couple of days, the straw would mash down to almost nothing.

Returning to the stables, we found a Corporal Jones

waiting for us. He welcomed us to A Company, 506 Regiment, 101st Airborne Division and briefed us on the situation around the camp, where to go, where not to go, how to act with the English and what would be expected of us. Then he showed us the "Screaming Eagle" patch, said that we would get them later from the supply room and told us to wear them with honor, for this was the shoulder patch of a great division. We were naturally curious about the history of the outfit and pumped the corporal with questions until he settled back on a bunk, gazed up through the cigarette smoke for a few moments as though reliving the past, then, with his slow Alabama drawl, told us about the regiment.

The 506 was activated July 20, 1942, at Camp Toombs, Georgia, later renamed Camp Toccoa. The men were all young, two-fisted, rough and tumble volunteers. The first step in separating the men from the boys was the famous "Three Mile Run." It consisted of running three miles to Mt. Currahee, three miles up the mountain, three miles down and three miles back to the starting place without stopping or slowing the pace. This total of twelve miles was run every morning before breakfast. Mt. Currahee became a symbol and an inspiration to the men who challenged it. An Indian name meaning "We stand alone," Currahee became the battle cry and motto of the regiment. For paratroopers landing deep behind enemy lines against overwhelming enemy forces truly had to "stand alone." The battle cry "Geronimo," used by the first experimental paratroopers in Africa, became the most well known of all battle cries, but did not take anything away from the others.

During the next few days the four of us from stable 13
became friendly, even Liddle loosened up, and in the evenings, sitting around talking, we learned as much about
each other as we knew about ourselves. Liddle was from
Utah, a Mormon, very quiet, non-drinking or -smoking and
without a nerve in his body. Phillips was from Pennsylva-
nia, Dutch descent, blond, blue-eyed and ready to do anything, any time, anywhere. Benson was a small man in
build, from Tennessee, dark straight hair, brown eyes, always intently watching others and an avid fan of crap
games. As for myself, I was from Michigan, 145 pounds,
dark hair, blue eyes and sometimes liked to go out raising
hell and at other times liked to lie around camp reading or
sketching pictures. Benson, Phillips and I were all eighteen. Phillips and I were so close to the same build that we
often wore each other's clothes. Liddle was larger than the
rest of us, and he was the oldest of the four—in his early
twenties, I think, he was one of the original group of men
that formed 506 at Camp Toombs, Georgia.

Later that week when all the replacements had arrived
and the regiment was considered to be up to full strength,
Colonel Bob Sink had us fall out, and from the hood of his
jeep gave us a speech of welcome. Colonel Bob is the type
of man that a person has to meet only once and will never
forget. A real man with plenty of guts, and more for the
enlisted man than any other officer I have ever known. He
also liked his whiskey and made sure that the men around
him had their share, whenever possible.

The new men blended into the outfit as though they
had always been there. For the rest of them, as for myself,
we now had an outfit, a home and a name, a feeling of

pride, belonging and brotherhood that all paratroopers
hold for each other.

Now the training started in earnest. The high command
had plans for us that we knew nothing of as yet, even
though everyone knew that some day we would spearhead
the invasion of Europe and soften the way for the infantry.
We practiced day and night assemblies over and over
again, until the difficult task of assembling large numbers
of scattered troopers under all conditions became second
nature and we could go through the whole procedure without anyone giving a single command. I was no longer a
machine gunner. This outfit already had machine gunners,
mortar and bazooka men. So I entered the second squad,
second platoon of A Company as a rifleman.

Spring was just around the corner, and one fairly warm
morning Phillips and I found ourselves on grenade loading
detail. First we had to fill the grenade shell about one-third
full of powder, then put a cap on the fuse and screw the
top onto the shell. I don't know who got the idea first, but
as it worked out we had hidden one can of powder and a
box of caps. When the detail was over we rummaged
around the company dump until we had gathered enough
after-shave powder cans to fill our needs, then filled them
with powder, put in a cap and replaced the lids. Taking an
armload each, we climbed to the roof of the stables, then
running the full length of the building we dropped a can
into every chimney we came to. We even dropped one into
our own to avert suspicion from us. The cans rattled down
into the fire pots. We knew that it would take a few moments for the heat to set the homemade bombs off and
this gave us time to get the job done and get off the roof.

The charges started going off and startled troopers came tumbling out of stables followed by billows of smoke. Then they were running back in throwing out smoking blankets and clothing onto the cobblestone courtyard. This was something we hadn't counted on. The charges were a little too heavy, and they peeled the stoves like bananas and cut the stovepipes off at the roof. Hot coals had been blasted over the insides of each stable, burning holes in clothing and blankets alike.

Later we found that the stoves had been loaned to us by the British and that we would be unable to get any replacements, so before the weather warmed up, we spent many nights wishing we had some kind of heat in the place. For weeks afterward, troopers were saying they wished they could get their hands on the ones who pulled that stunt. But this was a secret Phillips and I were both willing to keep.

The spring weather was unpredictable, wind one day, sunshine or rain the next, but still we had to keep in jump practice. We had simulated jumps but they weren't like the real thing. So one morning we got the word—a jump. It was scheduled for the next day so we had to spend this day getting ready for it. Machine guns had to be packed, rifles and mortars were rolled into packs and everything had to be in A-1 condition, ready to go.

Thomas, one of the men from the platoon, said that he was going to jump with a machine gun in his arms.

"If you can do it, so can I," I told him, and made a piece of webbing to tie around my squad machine gun and fasten to my harness.

Captain Davis told us that if it rained the jump would

be called off, and it did look a little cloudy when we loaded onto the trucks. But as we pulled onto Frox Field, the sky began clearing and a trooper sang "Blue Skies Shining for Me." We took off, flew around England for better than an hour, then made the drop. We hit the D.Z. and formed for the tactical problem. I was just getting out of harness when I heard a machine gun rattling on the field. "No one could have gotten a gun into action that quick," I thought. "I haven't got mine off the harness yet."

After we had assembled I heard officers and men talking about it. Thomas had unwrapped a belt of ammo from around the gun barrel after he got the opening shock, then, when he hit the ground, had opened the tripod, and while still in the harness, opened fire. This was a military first, and soon we would all be jumping steady with equipment. On this same jump T-5, Fleming had a man whose chute didn't open hit his canopy and come down so close that he reached out and caught hold of the other man's suspension lines. The weight of the man hurtling past tore the lines through Fleming's hands, cutting and burning deep into his flesh, but he held on. He held the man by the lines until the other man got his reserve open, then he turned him loose. They both landed safely.

The Captain announced that there would be a beer party in the community house, a building used by the civilians for meetings and social gatherings and for some of them, church on Sundays. Our party was scheduled for Saturday night. Barrels of beer were brought in, the whole company showed up, and each man did his best to outdrink the other. Things were getting woozy for me, and I only watched as a man broke the top out of a barrel and started eating the hops out of the bottom. Phillips and Benson helped me outside and were taking me back to the barracks when I told them I would rather lie down on the ground. It felt so cool and did more for clearing my head than anything else. That was the last thing I remembered.

Finally I woke up. Someone was talking and someone else was shaking my leg with a very firm hand. Raising my head, I looked out through heavy-lidded eyes onto a sea of blurry faces. Getting to my knees, I could see with a shock that three other troopers and myself were lying on the stage of the community house just behind a preacher who was blistering out a sermon on the wages of sin. It looked like Robbie who was shaking me, but I couldn't be sure; anyway we woke up the other troopers and crawled off the stage from behind the preacher on our hands and knees. It was kind of embarrassing.

There must be retribution though, for the next week we received new boots and most of us soaked them in water overnight and put them on the next morning so they would form to our feet as we wore them till they dried. We fell out for a hike, and Captain said it would be a short one, but before it was over we had hiked better than thirty miles. My feet hurt so bad that each step was torture. I knew they were blistered, but I didn't know how bad until we arrived back at the stables. Taking my boots off, I counted twenty-one blisters on my two feet. No wonder they hurt on the hike. Sitting on the edge of my bunk, I looked at the calendar on the wall. It was April 5th, my nineteenth birthday. Some present.

The time came for another jump, a night jump. Sergeant Vetland briefed us, and we went over the procedure of assembling and the importance of not making any noise once we were on the ground. The command was concerned about a strong wind coming up that night, and although they wanted this jump, they still did not want to take unnecessary chances. The word came down that we would maintain radio silence, and if we saw a fire on the jump field it would mean the wind had risen and the jump was canceled.

We loaded onto the planes and sat in the near darkness; the only light came from a small red bulb in the overhead. The takeoff was easy, and our flight of ships formed in the English skies. We flew for almost two hours, circling over the English countryside. The ride was a little rough at times, but on the whole, it was pretty smooth, and we sang songs and kidded each other about a coffee truck waiting on the D.Z. to serve us hot coffee when we landed. There were times in the past when our cooks were waiting on the D.Z. with hot coffee and sinkers, but these were on what we called parade-ground jumps. Sergeant Vetland suddenly said, "There's a fire on the jump field; we don't jump tonight."

I looked out the port and saw the dark shadow of another C-47 ghosting alongside us in the black skies. Suddenly tracers lanced through the air between us and them. Antiaircraft shells started bursting in fiery, short-lived flowers through our formation, sending their hot ragged steel seeds screaming outward to tear at the soft skins of our ship. The ship rocked and bounced under the impact of the exploding shells while we hung onto the safety straps of our bucket seats, wondering what the hell was going on.

One of the troopers yelled, "Packs out," and passed the

pack of cigarettes down the line. It came to me and I took one; the trooper on my left gave me a light and I inhaled deeply—it was my first cigarette. The crew chief appeared in the doorway of the cockpit; bracing himself against the sides of the opening he announced, "Be ready to go out on your reserve chutes, don't hook up. We have run into a Kraut bomber formation, and those fires down there are parts of London burning, so if you hear the claxon horn go off, don't wait to ask questions, just get out of the door as fast as you can." Brininstool was behind me, and I told him that I was scared. He laid a hand on my shoulder and said, "Don't worry, us guys from Michigan will stick together, remember, coffee and donuts when we hit the ground." The signal flashed on, the lead man yelled, "Let's go," and we were racing for the door to get out of the ship as fast as possible. I hit the prop blast and could hear the other chutes popping open in the night air, but everything was so dark that I couldn't make out a thing.

My opening shock never came and just as I reached for my reserve something soft and slippery billowed up around me. The next thing I knew was that I was in the top of someone's canopy. I yelled down for him not to slip, for I was riding his canopy and didn't want to slip off. If it were daylight and the ground visible we could have seen if we were high enough and I could have slid off the side of his chute and opened my reserve. But at night I didn't want to take the chance. I was in the top of his canopy when we hit the ground. The man below me hit first and the tension left his chute. It collapsed and I fell the twenty-two feet to the ground. The wind was knocked out of me, but otherwise I was unhurt. The man crawled to me and asked if I were O.K., and for a few moments I couldn't answer him, not until my breath returned. When we could see each other we both had a shock. It was Brininstool. He had jumped after me, and yet I landed in the top of his chute. This was impossible, yet it had happened.

We assembled in a quite orderly fashion and waited in company formations in the middle of a cutover hay field. A figure hung from a telephone pole, struggling to get free of his harness, and just as one of our group started to go to him we saw two other figures approach him.

One of the men on the ground asked, "Can I help you, trooper?"

"Yeh," the man on the pole said, "don't stand there like a damned fool, grab hold of the end of my jump rope and hold it still while I climb down." The man on the ground took hold of the rope dropped to him and held it tight. The trooper tied the other end to the saddle of his harness and slid to the ground, stood for a moment, then turned and ran toward us. We could see that it was Duffy. "Do you know who that was?" he blurted out. "That was General Ike. I didn't know it was him." Poor Duffy wasn't the same man for several days. He acted like a man waiting for the law to catch up to him.

When we returned to our camp we found that quite a few of our men were still missing. We thought they might be lying dead somewhere in a wrecked C-47. Then for the next ten days they came trickling into camp. Some of them had bailed out of disabled planes and had been taken prisoner by the English Home Guard and marched off to jail in front of pitchforks, shotguns and other weapons. Our jump suits were almost identical to the German paratroopers' and when the English found paratroopers dropping from the skies during a bombing raid they thought they were English-speaking German invasion forces. Finally word had gotten around, and through red tape and identification they were all finally released and returned. Some of the last ones to return weren't prisoners, though. They had landed in a fair-sized city and were recognized as Americans. The troopers seized the opportunity and checked their gear in at the Red Cross, then proceeded to paint the town red. They stayed at their little game until they heard through the grapevine that all the other troopers had returned except them. Only then did they return, bringing a wild tale of how they had been held all that time in a small town jail without communication and suddenly just released.

Soon the outfit moved to Torquay in southern England for maneuvers. The countryside there with its hedgerows resembled the Normandy coast and would be pretty close to what we would be fighting in. We were billeted in a large hotel overlooking the ocean. Our presence here was supposed to be a secret, and guards were placed on all the doors so we wouldn't go roaming around the city. None of us was allowed below the third floor except when we marched clear around the bay to the other side of the city for chow three times a day.

Our first day in the hotel was relaxing, but we wanted to move around a little, get a beer, do something besides just lie on our bunks. It was a warm sunny day and all the windows were open; troopers leaned out of them watching the surf wash up on the rocks of the beach. Phillips had crawled out onto a ledge just outside our window and was sitting there with knees drawn up under his chin, soaking in the warm sunshine. I crawled out beside him and we sat there for quite a while, not talking or doing anything in particular, just relaxing in the fresh spring air. People were passing by on the road running along the beach, some of them on bikes, others walking and a few of them in autos.

Before long a shapely young woman came walking down the road, but stopped when she came near the larger rocks across from the hotel. She looked around and waited until no one was in sight, then walked across the sand and stood between two of the larger rocks; she took off her shoes and put them with her purse on one of the stones, then waded into the water.

When she got about waist deep, Phillips said, "You know, I think she's going to commit suicide."

"Naw," I replied. "She wouldn't do that, not here in broad daylight."

She kept going, farther and farther, struggling against the surging water. We stood up and called to her, but it was too late, a large wave crashed over the rocks and she disappeared from sight. We never saw her again. Later we told our buddies about her, but no one would believe us, so we let the matter drop.

That same day we walked toward the front of the building where the officers were quartered and ran into a trooper who evidently had had too much to drink. We knew that was impossible, for no one could get out of here to get to a pub. When Phillips told him to cut out the drunk act, he lifted the canteen and told us to have a drink. It was good old English beer, every last drop of it. "Come on," he said. "I'll show you where you can get all you want, if you want to."

We fell in behind him and found ourselves sneaking through the officers' quarters and finally into the old man's private rooms.

"If we get caught in here," I reminded the other two, "we'll get nine years in the stockade."

"To hell with it," replied Phillips, "are you chicken?"

"No," I replied. "I didn't say I wanted out. I just wanted to make sure you two knew what we were in for if we got caught."

We went into the bathroom and locked the door behind us. The other trooper took a jump rope from his pocket and tied our three canteens to the end of it. "It was my idea," he announced, "so you guys buy." I handed him a ten-shilling note, and he put it on one of the canteens along with a note and went to the window which was directly over the hotel's pub entrance. Presently two English soldiers started into the doorway and we lowered the canteens in front of them. At first they walked around the containers inspecting them as though they might be booby traps. Finally they took the note and read it, looked up, smiled and disappeared with the containers into the building. A few minutes later they returned, tied the flasks onto the rope, thanked us and went back into the pub. We hauled the prize up and sat sprawled on the bathroom floor drinking the soul-warming beer. The note we had fastened to the canteens stated that the person filling the canteens with beer and retying them to the rope could have the balance of the change to buy their own drinks with. Time after time we lowered the rope to someone entering the pub and never once were we cheated out of a drink or our money. It seems that all the beer-drinking English were honest. I don't know about the churchgoers.

The next morning we fell out and were about halfway around the bay heading toward the mess hall when two small boats came roaring into the inlet. They headed straight for several larger ships tied up at the docks, and before we knew what was going on, they released torpedoes, made a wide sweeping turn and headed back out to sea. The torpedoes struck home, and two ships sank right where they sat at the docks. At first we stood awestruck, then most of us let out a cheer. It wasn't for the German victory, but rather for the way they had carried out the attack. Two small forces had entered the enemy's land, struck a death-dealing blow against overwhelming odds behind the lines and made good their escape. These hit-and-run tactics were what we had been schooled in, and this act seemed to be a symbol, a prophecy of what the future held in store for us. We couldn't help but cheer the display of sheer guts and bravery, despite the fact that it was committed by the enemy.

Later that day we moved by trucks to Honiton Airfield and were told that this was where we would take off from when the time came for us to go into combat. After being briefed on combat maneuvers, we boarded trucks and were scattered through the countryside as though we had jumped from planes. For several days we fought mock battles in the hedgerow country of southern England. Then we went back to Torquay and finally by truck convoy back to our base camp, Aldbourne.

Back in camp training, problems and maneuvers were

increased, and we had very little time to ourselves. Weapon inspections became daily routine until our equipment was in top condition, and night assembly practice after simulated jumps was pulled almost every night. On one field in particular we had dry run practice almost every night for a week. We knew the field like the back of our hands. We were told that two battalions would have to make a jump for Prime Minister Churchill and General Eisenhower. One battalion would have to stand inspection for the visiting officials. A coin was tossed and we, the first battalion, came out on top. We would be the ones to stay on the ground while the second and third made the jump.

The jump, witnessed by Prime Minister Churchill, General Eisenhower, General Bradley, General Taylor, General Pratt and General McAuliffe, was a success except for one equipment chute which had a streamer and pile-drived into the ground. As the unopened chute plummeted to the ground, the glider troops standing to our left turned and booed us, adding that they would take their chances in a glider any time. After the jump, Churchill called to us to assemble around the reviewing stand, which we did on a dead run. Then, with his daughter standing on his right, he spoke to us as only Churchill could speak. As we listened, we felt a great respect for this man, and we were honored to be in his presence.

This was our last practice jump before combat. In the next few days much of our personal equipment, bikes, lamps and so on was moved a little each night to the division dump and buried, so no one would suspect that we were getting ready to make a permanent move from this camp. Then we moved by trucks back to southern England. Once again we were in Torquay, but we didn't go to the hotel. We went straight to Upottery Airfield. This time it wasn't just for maneuvers and we all knew it. This was the wet run, the real thing.

We learned that beach landings would hit early in the morning of D-day, but that we, the airborne, would be dropped behind the Normandy Beaches several hours before. Many times during the briefings I noticed Cap de la Hague, the very tip of the Cherbourg Peninsula, pointing straight across the channel toward Honiton like an accusing finger. It was a good thing the Cap didn't also have a voice.

Our fenced-off area connected with the airfield, and Air Corps personnel manned our cook tents and mess halls and guarded the gates. We could have left the area any time we felt like it by slipping through the fence and sneaking past the guards, but we realized the importance of following orders and all the men behaved themselves.

The next few days were spent in briefing tents studying aerial photographs, maps and three-dimensional scale models of Normandy. Each paratrooper had to learn the whole operation by heart, know his own and every other outfit's mission to the most minute detail and be able to draw a map of the whole area from memory. We even knew that the German commandant of St. Côme-du-Mont owned a white horse and was going with a French schoolteacher who lived on a side street just two buildings away from a German gun emplacement. Troops wearing different German uniforms and carrying enemy weapons

roamed constantly through the marshaling area to familiar-
ize us with what the enemy looked like and what weapons
they carried.

One point made very clear to us was that although the
enemy had a strong coastal defense, they would rely heavily on large and mobile reserve units. These units would
wait in the background until some section of their frontal
defense was in danger of breakthrough, then speed to the
danger area, and after turning the tide of battle at that
point, return to reserve to wait for another threatened
breakthrough. It was therefore impressed on us very
strongly that regardless of where we were or how many
there were of us, if we came in contact with one of these
units we were to fire upon it with everything we had. If we
could detain any of these units, even for five minutes, it
might mean the difference between success or failure for
our troops or allies fighting at other strategic points.

Our main objectives were to take and hold all high
ground surrounding the areas of St. Côme-du-Mont,
Vierville and Ste. Marie-du-Mont and the cities themselves; capture or destroy the bridges crossing the rivers to
Carentan; capture the dikes above Carentan; and capture
and hold the four exits leading from the beach into the
interior, which would enable the troops landing from the
sea to get inland in a hurry without opposition once they
broke through the beach defenses. Exit 1 ran through
Pouppeville; exit 2, through Herbert; exit 3, through
Audoville-la-Hubert; exit 4, through St. Martin-de-
Varreville. We were also to cut all enemy communications,
block all roads, knock out enemy gun emplacements, raise
as much hell as possible and act as shock troops for our

infantry when they broke through to us. Furthermore, although the cutting of the underground telephone wires in the center of Ste. Mère-Église was one of the 82nd's objectives, it was such an important one we were told that if by some accident any of us found ourselves in or near Ste. Mère-Église, we were to do the job. At the end of 72 hours we were to be pulled out, leaving the mopping up for the ground troops.

On June 3rd, they issued each of us an escape·kit, consisting of a small compass, an unmarked map and seven dollars in French money. We were also issued a metal cricket apiece, one click being the challenge to anyone we met in combat and two the password to keep from getting one's head blown off. The verbal challenge for all airborne was "Flash," the password "Thunder," and if a man wasn't sure of who challenged him he could ask for the counter-sign "Welcome." The way to challenge a man is to draw a bead on him, wait until he is not more than fifteen or twenty feet away, then whisper, just loud enough for him to hear, the challenge word, "Flash." If he doesn't answer with the password or two clicks of the cricket, pull the trigger.

That night we sat sharpening knives, cleaning weapons and sorting through the personal things we figured we could or would need after the heavy fighting was over, like soap, shaving equipment and cartons of cigarettes. Phillips, Liddle, Benson, several other troopers and I were in the tent next to company headquarters with Captain Davis, Speedy West, the Teeter twins and some officers. It was raining that night, and all the canvas and blankets were wet, but we didn't mind, for most of us slept with our clothes on now, just removing our boots. After the usual joking and horseplay, things quieted down in the tent and we went to sleep.

Next morning was June 4, 1944, and we were still sitting in the heavy canvas tents waiting for the order to load on the planes that would carry us over to the coast of France. Rain had been falling all day and now it was coming down so hard that a trooper standing in it could hardly see the front sight of his rifle. The strong musty odor of tent canvas became stifling with the heavy humidity of the warm rain-laden June day. One bare electric light bulb hung from the tent's center post, casting grotesque shadows as the men moved about preparing their personal equipment and weapons on bare canvas cots. Some of the men were burning small piles of paper on the dirt floor, then smearing the cooled ashes on their hands and faces to blacken them for the coming night jump. Smoke from the fires thickened until we had water running from our eyes and nose; so we finished our tasks as quickly as possible, then lay on our cots where the air was clearer, closer to the ground.

We lay there talking and joking with each other and wondering what combat would really be like, when suddenly the talk in the next tent came into focus and we heard the Captain ask Speedy to play "San Antonio Rose" on his guitar.

The music sounded good, and we listened as we went about our small chores, but the request was repeated each time the song ended. Finally someone yelled at the Captain and asked if he wouldn't like to hear something else. He replied that he was from San Antonio and the plane he was riding in was also named that and he wanted to listen to that particular song until it was time to go.

The rain kept falling harder and harder through an increasing wind until it was coming down in torrential sheets and we thought for sure the whole operation would be called off. Suddenly a runner poked his head through the tent opening and said, "This is it, let's go."

We hit the outside on the double, and in columns of two started slogging our way toward the waiting planes. The ground was hard packed and grassless, and with the rain, the surface became slippery and slimy. Men kept sliding around until we got to the runways on the airfield; then it was easy walking, but still a long way to go. We found our assigned places at last, and looking and feeling like a bunch of half-drowned rats, we started to get ready. I was trying to get the wet parachute harness fastened while water ran into my eyes, off my nose and down my neck, every step bringing a squishy sound from my boots. All the extra equipment we had to carry didn't make the job any easier. Jeeps were running around the field on various errands looking like shadowy ghosts through the downpour of rain. One pulled up, spraying us with grit-filled water from under its wheels, and the driver said the operation was postponed until further notice. Some of us just stood there not knowing whether to feel relieved or mad, because we knew that we would have to go through the same thing again either tomorrow or the next day at the latest. Back in the tents most of us lay on the cots and slept the best way we could in the chill dampness of night, under single blankets from the packs we had made up to carry into combat with us.

The morning came bright and clear and started to warm up fast. Every man knew the invasion would start this day, June 5, 1944. The command was more lenient this day than they had been on any other occasion. The men were allowed to do just about as they pleased as long as they stayed in the compound. For afternoon chow we had fried chicken, all the trimmings and ice cream; we could have all we wanted; sort of a last meal. After chow the Captain had Speedy go through the guitar routine again, but this time it didn't last as long. Word came that coffee and donuts were being given out in the front area from trucks, and that they were free; no charge for them like the ones at the Red Cross. Phillips and I walked to the area through groups of other troopers and found the trucks. A small band was in one of the trucks blasting out a variety of tunes while the cooks doled out coffee and donuts. There was a large fire burning at the edge of the field and the men were going through the same routine of blackening their hands and faces with ashes raked from the fire and let cool. Some of the men were doing the Jolson bit, singing "Mammy," waving their hands and blinking white-looking eyes in blackened faces.

We were called to gather around a truck and General Taylor gave us a good luck speech. General Taylor recalled how General Bill Lee had said we had a "Rendezvous with Destiny," and he intended to see that we kept it. General Lee "invented" the Paratroops and tried in vain to get the U.S. government to put the idea into action but as usual some fat-assed chairborne officials voted against it. The Germans saw it for what it was and adopted General Lee's plans and put them to their own good use in Crete, Greece and Holland. Then the Russians started a paratroop division. Finally the U.S. opened their eyes and approved a paratroop unit in its original birthplace under the direction and command of General Bill Lee, "Father" of the Paratroops. After the 'Troops grew into several divisions, General Lee became the Commander of the 101st Airborne Division. But just before we were to go into combat he became ill and had to go to the hospital. General Taylor closed his speech by telling us to yell "Bill Lee" when we jumped into combat.

General Eisenhower was also there and was walking among the men talking to different ones and occasionally laughing at the answers he would get to his questions. Later we got ready all over again and marched the long distance to the other end of the field where our plane waited with what seemed to be hundreds of others. Phillips said, "This is always our luck, we draw the plane that's at the farthest end of the field. Just once I would like to get something real close, real fast or real easy."

Our heavy equipment was carried out on trucks and dumped on the ground in a pile. We started sorting through it to get the weapons, machine guns, mortars and shells that we would carry on the jump. Our rifles and personal gear we carried on the field ourselves. We also rolled paracks with bangalore torpedoes and other heavy equipment that would be carried on the outside belly of the plane and dropped in the middle of the stick by the crew chief.

"At least," Liddle said, "we didn't have to walk out here in mud like we did yesterday."

I asked Phillips if he would watch my gear while I went

to get more ammo for my .45. All machine guns and mortars would be carried on the persons of the gunners on this jump, but every man in the outfit would be required to carry a certain amount of ammo for one of these weapons. This way there would be a safe amount of ammunition for each weapon when we hit the ground. Other than the required weapons and ammo for them, we could carry whatever extra we wanted to. Great piles of grenades, ammo, explosives, and so on, were scattered about the place like mounds of hay on a cutover field.

Phillips was fastening his harness when I returned, but he had to lie face down to get the bellyband fastened. One trooper stood on his back while I cinched his strap; he was unable to get to his feet without help. A couple of Air Force men in coveralls walked up and told us they were assigned to help us wherever we needed them. One of them got on either side of Phillips and lifted him to his feet. He waddled to the plane but couldn't raise his foot high enough to get it on the step of the plane.

"Aw to hell with it," he said. "I'll stay here for a while." With that, he stood in a forward leaning position, looking as helpless as a diver in an over-inflated diving suit.

I started getting all my gear on, and just as I was reaching for my chute, Sergeant Vetland called to all of us and told us he had some pills we had to take. Hundley asked what they were and Vetland told him they were anti-motion pills so no one would get airsick on the flight.

"To hell with them," Hundley said. "I never get airsick anyway so I'm not going to take them."

"The hell you won't," Vetland said. "Everyone takes

them and that's an order. You will take one every half hour, starting now."

We lined up and he counted out nine of them and stood there while the trooper took his first one and washed it down with a swig from his canteen. When he reached me and counted out the right amount into my hand I examined them, and to this day I still don't know what they really were. We never received anti-motion pills on any jump before or since then. They were about the size of a paper match head, cylindrical in shape and pure white.

"Come on," Vetland said. "We haven't got all day, eat the damned thing."

I popped the pill into my mouth and swallowed, but it stuck in my throat so I took a big slug of water like the other men down the line were doing, but instead of going down it seemed to swell when the water hit it, and the harder I swallowed the tighter it seemed to stick.

"If it ain't one damned thing it's another," I thought, anything to make a man a little more uncomfortable; and I went back to getting my gear on.

My personal equipment consisted of: one suit of O.D.s, worn under my jump suit—this was an order for everyone—helmet, boots, gloves, main chute, reserve chute, Mae West, rifle, .45 automatic pistol, trench knife, jump knife, hunting knife, machete, one cartridge belt, two bandoliers, two cans of machine gun ammo totaling 676 rounds of .30 ammo, 66 rounds of .45 ammo, one Hawkins mine capable of blowing the track off of a tank, four blocks of TNT, one entrenching tool with two blasting caps taped on the outside of the steel part, three first-aid kits, two morphine needles, one gas mask, a canteen of water, three days' supply of K rations, two days' supply of D rations (hard tropical chocolate bars), six fragmentation grenades, one Gammon grenade, one orange smoke and one red smoke grenade, one orange panel, one blanket, one rain-coat, one change of socks and underwear, two cartons of cigarettes and a few other odds and ends.

Other things would be dropped in equipment bundles that we would pick up later on the ground: bangalore tor-pedoes, extra bazooka rockets, machine-gun ammo, medi-cal supplies, food and heavy explosives.

Charlie Syer, our bazooka man, carried the new-type bazooka. It came unjointed in the center and fit into a canvas bag in two short pieces. This new one was fired by a small generator built into the handle instead of the flash-light batteries of the old one. Jackson, Montrella and the other mortar men carried their mortars in canvas bags fas-tened to their legs by web straps and wires. A twenty-foot jump rope ran from the pack to the saddle of the harness. After receiving the opening shock, the mortar man would pull the wire allowing the bundle to fall free of his leg and hang suspended twenty feet below him on the end of the jump rope tied to his saddle. This way he could jump with the mortar, yet be free of its weight when he hit the ground. Carter and the other machine gunners carried two cans of ammo in special canvas bags strapped on either side of their hips. They carried the guns in their arms with half a belt of ammo wrapped around the barrel, ready to fire the moment they hit the ground. Most of the riflemen carried their weapons in padded gun cases strapped under their reserve chutes. The rifles were taken apart and had to be assembled after the trooper hit the ground.

I got everything set except for the fastening of my belly-band, and when I tried to lie down, I found it impossible to bend at the waist and had to fall into a prone position, breaking the fall with my hands. The two Air Corps men came up and asked if I needed any help. I told one of them to stand on my back while the other fastened the belly-band; after which I found it impossible to even get to my knees. The two men lifted me bodily, and with much boosting and grunting shoved me up into the plane where I pulled myself along the floor and with the aid of the crew chief got into a bucket seat. When all the troopers were aboard, a loudspeaker came on and the pilot read us a mimeographed message from General Ike, wishing us luck and Godspeed. "A canteen cup of whiskey would have been more appreciated," I thought.

The pilot revved the engines, checking the mags, oil pressure and other instruments and controls. The feathered props slapped the air making popping noises and at times getting louder, then softer, like the sound of a car driving behind a row of houses. The plane shook and vibrated as the air from the props rushed by on each side of the fuselage. It seemed as though the big machine, eager to take off, was straining against an invisible leash.

It was time for another pill and all the men took them, as far as I knew. After that third one I felt as though I had taken about three double shots of whiskey on an empty stomach. Even the noises of the vibrating, rattling skin of the plane faded away and the interior of the plane took on a drowsy comfortable air. We closed the door. This was the first time we ever had a door on the plane and it gave us sort of a cooped-up feeling. The crew chief gave the order to put out all smokes and we taxied into position, waited our turn, then went roaring down the runway.

The plane rose heavily. Looking out the port I could see the wings bow and then come back to their original place.

"Flap your wings, you big-assed bird," I yelled.

The ship nosed down to gain speed and for a moment it looked as though we would never live to see combat for we were heading straight for a row of tall trees. At the last moment the pilot pulled up and we were in the clear, heading toward the vast formation gathering in the English skies. The last thing I really remember seeing on the ground was a large haystack made of bales of hay and thatched like a house to keep the rain off.

We had so much equipment on and were so uncomfortable that the best way to ride was to kneel on the floor and rest the weight of the gear and the chutes on the seat itself. The airborne had repeatedly requested the presence of a journalist or cameraman to accompany us into combat. The requests were refused by all journalists and photographers except for one who didn't jump but who did make the round trip in one of the planes. Later I read an account by this reporter. He wrote that we were knelt in prayer. Actually, it was just a comfortable way to ride. After taking the pills I felt a happy glow on and at peace with the world and even managed to sleep a little during the flight.

3

COMBAT

IT WAS STILL LIGHT WHEN WE TOOK OFF, BUT night came while we assembled over England. Now our wing lights were on and the inside of the ship was lit by little red lights overhead. Sixteen other troopers sat or knelt on either side of the plane, some of them smoking, the ends of their cigarettes glowing white in the dim red light of the plane. The plane bounced and rocked, for we were coming in at a low altitude. Then the crew chief came walking back in a halting, staggering fashion, bracing himself against the roll of the ship. He told Lieutenant Muir that we were approaching enemy territory and had better get ready. The Lieutenant ordered us to remove the door and to stand up and hook up, the coast of France was just ahead. The troopers had been singing different songs, including "Blood Upon the Risers," but now we were all quiet, listening for commands.

General Taylor had given orders for all the men to be standing when we hit enemy territory; he claimed that if any trooper got hit he wanted him to be standing and take

it like a man. If I were going to get a chunk of flak through the guts I didn't care if I were standing or sitting. Actually there was a practical reason for this order; if a plane got hit, the men hooked up and ready to jump would stand some chance of getting out.

We made the run around the Cherbourg Peninsula, then, making a sharp left turn, we flew over and between the islands Jersey and Guernsey and headed toward the Normandy Beach from the back side. Fires were burning on the ground, a result of the bombers that had preceded us in. Their mission was to try and knock out heavier gun emplacements and to give the Germans the impression that this was just another bombing raid.

The plane rose and fell under the impact of bursting antiaircraft shells. Sometimes it felt as though a giant hand had slapped the ship sideways. The plane would shudder, then come back to level flight under the working hands of the pilot. I was standing near the open door of the plane and could see the tracers, flak bursts and what appeared to be rockets screaming up through the black night. The night air was filled with thousands of strings of fiery tracers winding their follow-the-leader, snakelike pattern up through the skies.

There are four armor-piercing bullets between each two tracers, I thought, "how the hell can anything get through here in one piece?" A quick ticking sounded as a string of machine-gun bullets walked a fast line of holes across our left wing. Large pieces of flak chunked through the ship every once in a while, but there seemed to be a constant pinging of smaller pieces that would pierce the metal, then ricochet from wall to wall as though looking for an escape. A couple of times I heard a grunt and I knew the shrapnel had hit someone.

We had our static lines hooked to the anchor cable and were hanging onto them for support in the bouncing ship. Garter and Thomas were on either side of the equipment bundle in the doorway ready to push it out on signal, while Lieutenant Muir clung to the web straps of the bundle to be carried out with it. It seemed like an eternity, riding through this fiery sky. Standing near the door, all I could think of was how beautiful and immense all the fireworks were. But where was it all coming from, for the Germans seemed to have an endless supply of it?

The time was 1:14 A.M. June 6, 1944. Suddenly the green light flashed on.

"Let's go," screamed Lieutenant Muir at the top of his voice, and he, along with Carter and Thomas, gave the big bundle a shove. Lieutenant Muir followed it out; Garter did a quick left turn and followed him into the prop blast; Thomas did a right turn and followed Garter. I could see their static lines snap tight against the edge of the door and vibrate there with the force of the outside wind pulling on them.

"Go," a voice screamed in my brain, "hurry!" Speed was the most important thing now, so we would all land as close together as possible. Everything seemed to be moving in slow motion again, but I knew that it was really happening in just fractions of seconds as I made my right turn into the door and with a left pivot leaped into dark space.

There were thirteen men following me out the door, but I couldn't see any of them. Doubled up and grasping my reserve chute, I could feel the rush of air, hear the crackling of the canopy as it unfurled, followed by the sizzling suspension lines, then the connector links whistling past the back of my helmet. Instinctively the muscles of my body tensed for the opening shock, which nearly unjointed me when the canopy blasted open. From the time I left the door till the chute opened, less than three seconds had elapsed. I pulled the risers apart to check the canopy and saw tracer bullets passing through it; at the same moment I hit the ground and came in backward so hard that I was momentarily stunned.

I lay on my back shaking my head; the chute had collapsed itself. The first thing I did was to draw my .45, cock
the hammer back and slip the safety on. Troopers weren't
issued pistols, but my father had purchased this one from a
gun collector in Detroit and sent it to me in a package
containing a date and nut cake. Captain Davis kept it in his
possession for me and let me carry it on field problems. He
had returned it to me when we entered the marshaling
area.

The pilots were supposed to drop us between 600 and
700 feet, but I know that my drop was between 250 and
than 300 feet. The sky was lit up like the Fourth of July. I
lay there for a moment and gazed at the spectacle. It was
awe inspiring, I have never seen anything like it before or
since. But I couldn't help wondering at the same time if I
had got the opening shock first or hit the ground first; they
were mighty close together.

The snaps on the harness were almost impossible to
undo, and as I lay there on my back working on them,
another plane came in low and diagonally over the field.
The big ship was silhouetted against the lighter sky with
long tongues of exhaust flame flashing along either side of
the body. Streams of tracers from several machine guns
flashed upward to converge on it. Then I saw vague, shadowy figures of troopers plunging downward. Their chutes
were pulling out of the pack trays and just starting to un-
furl when they hit the ground. Seventeen men hit the
ground before their chutes had time to open. They made a
sound like large ripe pumpkins being thrown down to
burst against the ground.

"That dirty son of a bitch of a pilot," I swore to myself,

"he's hedgehopping and killing a bunch of troopers just to save his own ass. I hope he gets shot down in the Channel and drowns real slow."

There wasn't any sense in going to those men, for I had seen the results of men hitting the ground with unopened chutes before. If by some miracle one of them were still alive, he would be better off to be left alone to die as quickly as possible; it would be more merciful.

By this time I was free of my harness, had my rifle assembled and loaded, and had crawled to my canopy. Gutting a panel out with my knife, I stuffed it into a pocket to use for camouflage later, then started out to find someone else, anyone else. More planes went over, but they were flying so low, fast and scattered that it was impossible to orient myself with their direction. I would have to play this one by instinct. In fact, all the troopers would have to do it this way. We were so widely scattered that all the months of practiced assemblies in the dark were shot in the ass. We would have to do this one on our own.

The night was one of those mild June nights that poets write about, but this was neither the time nor the place for poetry. There was the booming of antiaircraft guns and mortars all around and the close stitching of German light and heavy machine guns raking the skies and hedgerows. Small arms fire erupted everywhere and sometimes it broke out hotter than the hinges on hell's gates in one spot. It would rise in ferocity until the fire power became a loud roar, then gradually taper off, sometimes even coming to a complete silence. I could see a mental picture of a few paratroopers running into a German fortification and fighting until they either took the place or died trying.

Small private wars erupted to the right and left, near and far, most of them lasting from fifteen minutes to half an hour, with anyone's guess being good as to who the victors were. The heavy hedgerow country muffled the sounds, while the night air magnified them. It was almost impossible to tell how far away the fights were and sometimes even in what direction. The only thing I could be sure of was that a lot of men were dying in this nightmarish labyrinth. During this time I had no success in finding anyone, friend or foe. To be crawling up and down hedgerows, alone, deep in enemy country with a whole ocean between yourself and the nearest allies sure makes a man feel about as lonely as a man can get.

The ground felt like grazed-over pasture, the short grass was wet with dew or a light rain, soaking my knees and elbows. Suddenly, just as I was about to enter a small willowy growth about eight feet high and twenty feet across, I heard a noise that was made by someone crawling on their hands and knees. My throat went dry and I swallowed, but nothing went down. My heart pounded, sending blood throbbing through my temples and causing a weak feeling in the pit of my stomach. Cold sweat dripped from under my armpits and trickled down my arms. The palms of my hands were covered with sweat. I rubbed them slowly, gently on the wood stock of my rifle to dry them, then eased into a prone position. I reached in a pocket and brought out the metal cricket that had been issued to each man. Placing it along the left side of the rifle barrel, I clicked it once with my thumb as a challenge while I kept a bead on the spot where the noise came from.

No reply came and I took up the slack in the trigger,

but then waited. I didn't want to shoot and find out too late that it had been the only friend in the area. Yet I didn't want to be killed either. Well, this is it, I thought, "He didn't give any answer to my challenge. I'll try him once more; if he doesn't answer, he's going to die." The cricket clicked again and this time a figure emerged from the thicket on hands and knees and moved unsteadily toward me. I had the drop on him, so I figured that even if it were a Kraut, he was my prisoner; if he made one false move at this point I could blow his head off.

The figure was about six feet away and suddenly I knew him; "Hundley, you dumb son of a gun, why in the hell didn't you answer me?"

He answered that he had lost his cricket and his throat was so dry he couldn't say the password. He knew if he tried to run I would kill him. His only chance was to get close enough to be recognized. We lay there taking small swigs from our canteens, swishing the water around our mouths before swallowing it.

"Do you know where in the hell we're at?" he asked.

"No," I answered, "but if we make our way toward some of the heavy shooting, we should find some of our buddies, and from the sounds of it they could use our help."

At this moment we both saw two crouched figures moving toward us from across the field.

"You take the left and I'll take the right," I whispered, and this time, instead of using the cricket, I whispered the challenge, "Flash"; the reply, "Thunder," came back in a hurry. The two figures joined us and turned out to be Slick Hoenscheidt and Red Knight. They said they could hear us whispering clear across the field. The four of us decided to find a place where we could defend ourselves and rest until daybreak, when we would stand a better chance of finding friendly troops without running into an army of enemy.

"There's a clump of trees over in that direction," said Slick, pointing with his rifle; "maybe we can hole up there."

We started crawling in single file and came across a ditch that ran toward the trees. Red, up front, stopped and said that he would just as soon stay in the ditch until morning. I crawled up to him and reminded him of the briefing we had in the marshaling area, when they told us that the Krauts had had several years to prepare range cards for every ditch in Europe and that we would stand a better chance almost any place else than in a ditch that they were sure to work over with mortar shells.

"That's right," he agreed. "Wait here a few minutes while I scout ahead; no sense in all of us getting shot up."

Red disappeared on hands and knees in the dark and we waited impatiently for his return. He came back the same way he had gone and was pretty happy about a big hole he had found near the edge of the trees. It had water in it, but there was plenty of room around the bottom edges for several men to lie down. We followed Red down the ditch and into the big hole, settling down to wait for daybreak and a chance to orient ourselves. A Kraut machine gun ripped a long burst toward us and we watched the tracers tearing through the trees just over our heads and felt the shower of twigs and bark rain down on us. Another burst raked the edge of the hole sending a cloud of dirt into our faces. Then Hundley said in his soft southern drawl, "They know where we're at, now all they have to do is get a tree burst with a mortar shell over our heads and we'll be driven into the bottom of this hole like hamburger."

"That settles it," said Slick. "We've got to make a break for it and go back the way we came."

One at a time we left the hole between machine-gun bursts and made it back to the ditch. Here we regrouped and then I noticed the shell marks spaced evenly along the bottom and called the others' attention to them. A mortar shell exploding on hard ground just leaves a small spiderweb mark, no bigger than a man's hand, but the concussion and fragments are terrific. If we stayed in that ditch we would be blown to bits too.

Again we moved out in single file, but this time in the opposite direction, following the hedgerows, looking for a good spot to hole up. We came across a small two-wheeled cart loaded with mortar shells and still attached to a parachute. We buried the whole thing in the side of a hedgerow, figuring to retrieve it later when we contacted more troops. As it turned out, we never did return to this spot, and as far as I know that cart with the mortar shells is still buried there. Moving down by a hedge to our right we came to a place that afforded cover and decided to stay there until daylight.

A misty rain started falling. We moved farther under the hedge, but soon water collected on the leaves and large drops began soaking us. Taking turns sleeping and guarding we spent the last hours huddled against the side of the hedge and at long last the sky turned a cold grey in the first

T-5 Assembly parachute practice jump. Men learn to jump and use the chute that will take us into combat in later days. *(Mark Bando)*

More than one way to collapse a chute after landing. This trooper runs into the chute until the lines go slack, then runs around the canopy and it will simply collapse. *(Mark Bando)*

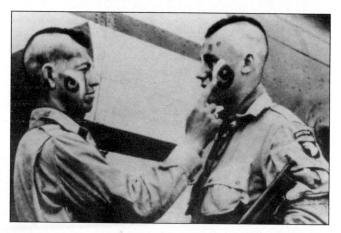

Warriors into combat. Some paratroopers went the extra step to strike fear in the enemy. These two, as did others, sport their "Geronimo" scalp locks with pride along with their war-paint faces. Later orders forbade the practice due to Nazi propaganda that these men were all convicted killers. *(Signal Corps)*

Rare photograph of members of second platoon, Co. A, 506 Parachute Regiment, 101ˢᵗ Airborne, emplaning the evening of June 5, 1944, for the D-day jump. We jumped at 01:14 on June 6, landing near Ravenoville, France, 12 miles from our drop zone. I am circled. *(Signal Corps)*

Warrior leaps from C-47. Trooper Joe Okeskewicz with tommy gun, Mae West, painted face, and scalp lock ready to jump into combat. Note the left foot forward and the hand outside the door. Basic form for military jump. *(Signal Corps)*

Over the English Channel, on the way to Normandy. These heavily laden paratroopers, although uncomfortable, managed to get a little sleep. The nearest trooper shows a map case on his side and a gas mask fastened to his leg. *(Mark Bando)*

No greater price. This paratrooper paid the full price so that all may live in freedom. He was killed on June 6, 1944, in Normandy. Grateful French citizens buried him with honors. His body was later moved to a military cemetery, where a small corner of France will forever be America. *(Ed Benecke)*

Suspected Nazi big-gun emplacements near the coastal edge of Normandy caused American aerial and naval bombardment to reduce this forest to devastation. I recall walking through here on June 7, 1944, and it was like walking through hell itself. *(Ed Benecke)*

Pillbox loser. This German pillbox near Utah Beach outside Ravenoville lost a shoot-out battle against American gunners. This pillbox is merely a fixed gun turret of a much larger fortified complex underground. Note the shell marks and bullet strikes. *(Ed Benecke)*

Banana split. Ed Benecke's gun crew of the 377th Parachute Field Artillery spiked this German gun with a bangalore torpedo down the tube, peeling the barrel back like a banana. Near Ravenoville and Utah Beach. *(Ed Benecke)*

Passing German dead on our march to St. Côme-du-Mont. I am shown on far right, along with Paul Carter and Prentice Hundley following. (Both were later killed in Holland.) Note the German potato-masher grenades in my belt front and a first-aid kit tied to my helmet. (*U.S. Army*)

Scratch one sniper or spotter. The first thing the Americans or Germans did when taking a town was to blow the steeple off the church, which usually held an artillery observer or an enemy sniper. (*Ed Benecke*)

The French Resistance moved street signs around along with the name signs of towns and villages to confuse the Germans. The Germans took to painting the real names of towns on prominent buildings to combat this practice. *(Ed Benecke)*

The quick and the dead. Bodies of German soldiers killed in one of our clashes were gathered in a field where our Graves Registration Team checked their ID tags, made records, and saw to it that they had a decent burial. Near St. Côme-du-Mont. *(Ed Benecke)*

The steel gate. After our successful attack into Carentan, the gate that stood across the Carentan Causeway over the Douve River was torn down and dragged by jeep into the entrance of Carentan, where it was left standing next to the city's sign. The troopers to the left still keep a wary eye out for Germans. (*Mark Bando*)

Battle-tested squad leader. Sgt. Brininstool was my squad leader for most of my combat time. He was sharp, cool, and a hell of a destroyer of the enemy. Brininstool's signature is on photo. (*Mark Bando*)

light of the false dawn. The rain had stopped but water dripped from the rims of our steel helmets as we peered over the hedge and scanned the countryside for some familiar landmark memorized in our preinvasion briefing. A lone church steeple stood silhouetted against the lighter part of the sky to our left front. We knew instinctively that all the able troopers in the area would head for it. We heard the sound of airplanes, and, looking up, saw several American B-17 bombers flying high, heading inland on a bombing mission.

German antiaircraft went into action and small puffs of black smoke appeared in the sky, showering deadly hunks of hot steel through the air. What appeared to be rockets, like the ones I had seen during our flight in, exploded in a long row in front of and above the formation. Parts of the burning "rockets" hung high in the sky while flaming particles rained down, forming a huge showering curtain of flame through which our bombers had to pass. One of the planes caught fire and four chutes came out in a hurry. The planes passed through a second wall of fire, the stricken ship exploded and fell in three huge separate sheets of flame. The four men drifting down were too far away for us to go to their aid, so we turned away and started toward the church steeple.

We crossed a few hedgerows and came to a road. Slick cautiously poked his head through the brush, then, without warning, leaped on through calling for us to follow him. We did and found ourselves on a dirt country road facing a group of troopers who looked as glad to see us as we were to see them. Some of them wore patches of the 82nd and some of the 101st. In the grey light I could see their sweat-streaked blackened faces and wondered if mine was as streaked as theirs. Lieutenant Muir stepped from the group and asked how many of us there were.

"Just the four," I replied.

"Swell," he said, "there's seven of us here; we're going to attack that town; you can come along if you want."

"Sure, Lieutenant, we were going that way anyway," I said.

Lieutenant Muir put Nick and Archie as scouts and put me as connecting link between them and the main body. Muir gave the command and we moved out. Nick and Arch were about a quarter mile in front of the main body with me about middle ways, so I could watch them and the men behind me at the same time. The sun, shining brightly now, was just peeking over the edge of the horizon. This was almost like a stroll down a country lane back home in the summertime, except for the sporadic fighting going on around us just out of our reach. Green leaves covered the trees and the road became dusty as the sun dried the moisture off the surface.

We moved along for about a half a mile without incident. Suddenly the road made a bend to the left and the scouts in front disappeared from my view. After rounding the bend and seeing the road straighten out to where I should have been able to see Nick and Arch, I called the main group to a halt. For the road ahead was empty. The Lieutenant came running up and asked what the trouble was. When I explained it to him he told me to look over the hedgerows and fields for them and the rest of the men would cover me. The first field I entered on the left had a tall pole in the center, with long strings of barbed wire

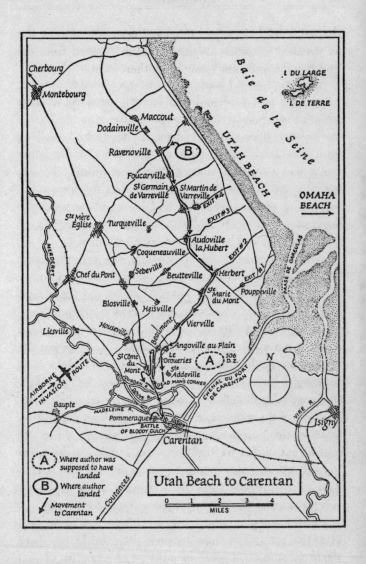

Cherbourg

Montebourg

Baie de la Seine

I. DU LARGE

I. DE TERRE

Maccout

Dodainville

Ravenoville

B

UTAH BEACH

Foucarville

St Germain de Varreville

St Martin de Varreville

EXIT #4

OMAHA BEACH

EXIT #3

Ste Mère Eglise

Turqueville

Audoville la Hubert

EXIT #2

MERDERET R.

Coqueneauville

Sebeville

Chef du Pont

Beutteville

Herbert

EXIT #1

Pouppeville

PASSE DE GRANDCAMP

Ste Marie du Mont

Blosville

Heisville

Vierville

Liesville

Houseville

N

Beaumont

Angoville au Plain

St Côme du Mont

Le Dr—ueries

506 D.Z.

A

Ste Addeville

AIRBORNE INVASION ROUTE

JOURDAN R.

DEAD MAN'S CORNER

CHEMIN DU PORT DE CARENTAN

DOUVE R.

Baupte

MADELEINE R.

Pommerague

VIRE R.

Isigny

BATTLE OF BLOODY GULCH

Carentan

A — Where author was supposed to have landed

B — Where author landed

→ Movement to Carentan

Coutances

Utah Beach to Carentan

0   1   2   3   4

MILES

stretched from the top and extending outward to the
ground, like the spokes of a wheel, or a maypole. "This," I
thought, "was put here strictly for our benefit." Can you
imagine what would happen to a trooper coming down at
twenty-two feet a second and landing astraddle a sharp
string of barbed wire forty feet above the ground? Then I
saw the two rifles and packs lying on the ground. Walking
over, I nudged a pack with my toe and saw the name
Ponds and a serial number written on it in ink. The sick
feeling came back deep inside my stomach, for this was the
equipment of our two scouts and here I was standing in
the center of an open field with enough shrubbery around
the outer edges to hide a company of riflemen.

What happened to the two men, where were they, why
hadn't they fired a shot? All these questions filled my mind
as I wondered what move I should make. Not knowing if
there were enemy eyes watching or how many guns were
trained on me, I turned, as if the things on the ground
didn't mean a thing to me, and strolled back toward the
edge of the field expecting with every step to feel the hard
slapping of bullets tearing through my body. But I made it
to the edge and walked through the gate onto the road.
The rest of the men returned to the field with me and we
searched the surrounding area, but no trace of the two was
ever found until after the war when Ponds was returned
from a prisoner-of-war camp. Although Nick and Archie
were taken prisoner together, the two became separated
and no trace of Nick has ever been found to this day.

We reformed on the road, and this time Lieutenant
Muir told me I would have to scout alone, for he could not
afford more men. I took up position of scout, about 300

yards ahead of the rest of the men, and started on down the road. I felt lonely up there and kept glancing back to see if the rest of the men were still behind me. The road made a long gradual curve back to the right. Up till now we hadn't passed any houses or enemy positions that I knew of. Soon we came to a town, but the sign bearing the town's name was missing so we still didn't know where we were at. The buildings and town were of medieval design, grey stone houses, barns and sheds built onto and leaning against each other and scattered about haphazardly. Narrow streets wound in and out between buildings that were sometimes connected by stone walls. The place was a natural fortress and could have been filled with enemy troops, so I signaled for the men behind me to halt and wait until I looked around.

Just then three young girls, about eighteen or so, came out of a doorway and ran to me yelling, "Vive les Américains."

Then, with a lot of hugging and kissing, they offered me a jug of wine, which I refused. Not that I don't like wine, but I just didn't feel like being poisoned, and at this time I didn't trust anyone. The Lieutenant had arrived by this time and asked if anyone could speak English. The girls said, in very poor English, that there was an old woman who could; she used to teach it in school. One of the girls brought her to us. Muir asked her where we were, and even though she told us we still didn't know. The Lieutenant brought his map out and the old woman pointed to the coastal town, "Ravenoville," and told us there were other Americans here, but also many Germans all around and even in the town itself. We thanked her, then Lieutenant

Muir cussed and swore as he examined the map, for we were about twelve miles from our drop zone and our objectives. Muir let out a string of oaths that ended with the Air Corps; "They dropped us all over the whole damned Cherbourg Peninsula," he said. "Who the hell's side are they on anyway? Now we've got to fight through nine towns and twelve miles of enemy country just to get to where we were supposed to land and start fighting in the first place."

We took up our formation again, and still in the role of scout, I led the way up the hill toward the center of town. Coming to the crest, I stopped to look the situation over before signaling the rest of the men to move up. There was a trooper lying in the ditch on the left side of the road, and when he looked my way I recognized him as Thomas. The place looked pretty quiet so I leaned against a large tree and lit a cigarette. Taking a deep drag and savoring the flavor, I looked down the road and saw where another one crossed it at the base of the hill. Just then a bullet slapped into the tree next to my head, but I figured it was just a stray from all the shooting going on around us. I continued to enjoy the cigarette. It was my first since we jumped. Another bullet slapped into the tree, a little closer this time, and Thomas said, "You had better get down; a Kraut has been sniping at every one that shows himself since early this morning."

"Why in the hell didn't you tell me?" I asked, as I slid into a sitting position behind a tree. He replied that he didn't know if the Kraut was still there and the only way to find out was to let me stand there for a while and see if I got shot at.

Lieutenant Muir came up and asked me what the score was. "Ask him," I said, pointing to Thomas. "He's been here longer than I have."

The Lieutenant asked him if there were any more troopers around and he said, "Sure, there's about eight or nine of us here."

"Any officers?" queried the Lieutenant.

Thomas nodded his head and told Muir that he would find a couple in the stone house across the field. Muir said thanks and started walking toward the building. When he'd gotten about halfway there, a machine gun hidden at the far end of the field burst out in a long fast chatter and clouds of dust rose around the Lieutenant's feet. For a moment he was too stunned to do anything but look pop-eyed at Thomas. A second burst sent him into a dancing jig as bullets ricocheted around his feet and went whining and screaming in different directions.

"You dirty son of a bitch," screamed Lieutenant Muir, as he saw Thomas rolling on the ground with laughter. "You knew that German was there."

The humor was catching and I lay on the ground next to Thomas laughing till my sides hurt. A third machine-gun burst and Muir was running hell bent for election toward the stone house. He made it O.K., and Thomas told me that Kraut couldn't hit the broad side of a barn and that he himself had made several trips across the same field under the same conditions.

"You're a regular joker, aren't you?" I asked. We both started to laugh again. The Lieutenant sure was funny.

A few minutes later Lieutenant Muir appeared in a doorway to the house, then, lowering his head, he came pounding across the field amid bursts of machine-gun fire and slid into the ditch with us.

"The rest of the town from this point on is a German fortress," the Lieutenant said. "If you'll notice, you can see catwalks in the treetops."

Looking up I saw boardwalks with side railings running through the treetops and covering most of this half of town. "For crying out loud," I thought, "they could run through those trees like a bunch of squirrels and watch every move we made getting here."

The Lieutenant sent me out to round up all the men I could find and bring them to him for a briefing. I found the troopers Thomas told me about in an apple orchard. Among them were Justo and Phillips. Then, along with the men who had come into town with me, we returned to Lieutenant Muir. There were seventeen men and three officers.

"Hell, that's plenty to take over this place," he said.

"After all, that's what we came here for, to kill Krauts and from the looks of it, there are plenty to go around."

"What's your plan?" one of the men asked.

After a little thought the Lieutenant answered, "A head-on attack and the sooner the better, so let's go." He jumped up and started running toward the group of houses across the field, yelling as he went. We all jumped up and followed him, yelling and screaming at the top of our lungs. We automatically spread out and fired as we ran through the fields, apple orchards and right up to the houses themselves. I saw my first Kraut running through the trees on an angle toward our right flank. I stopped, took a good sight on him and squeezed the trigger. The rifle bucked against my shoulder. I don't remember hearing the shot or feeling the recoil, but the German spun sideways and fell facefirst out of sight in the grass. Another Kraut stepped around the corner of a building, stopped and just stood there looking down at the spot where the first soldier fell. He was facing me. I had a good straight-on shot at his chest and took careful aim. Again the rifle bucked against my shoulder, and he too fell face forward.

Fighting was at a fever pitch now. All around, men were running between buildings, through yards and over fences. Four troopers ran through a gate in a hedge surrounding a house and almost immediately there came a long ripping burst of a Kraut machine gun. The four Americans died in the weed-choked front yard. Automatically other troopers shunned the yard but moved on the double on all fours down the hedges on either side until they were in throwing distance of the house and grenaded it. One trooper leaped through a side window, fired several rounds from his M-1, then stepped to the front door and motioned that it was all clear. Running through the open gateway, past the dead and into the house, I saw a German machine gun, a lot of empty shells and a couple of boxes of ammo under the window to the left of the door. No Germans or bodies were in the house. Evidently they had cleared out when the first grenades hit, leaving their gun behind. The trooper who went through the window said they went out the back way just as he entered. He fired at them but none of them went down. We left the house and rejoined the others in clearing out the remaining houses.

Two troopers came out of one of the buildings carrying a case of German hand grenades between them. They ran down the street throwing the potato mashers into windows and apertures in the walls. German soldiers were pulling out of town by the back way and disappearing into fields and woods surrounding the town. German dead were scattered about in the houses, ditches and fields. I don't know how many I hit. The ones who fell when I fired would have dropped anyway if a bullet had passed close to them.

After occupying the enemy positions we wondered why they had given them up so easily, for the walls were all of stone and two feet thick, with small rifle apertures to fire out from, and many of the rooms were filled with food, ammo and weapons. Over 200 Germans had vacated these positions, leaving behind thirty dead and about seventy-five prisoners. Four of our men had been killed. Phillips could speak some German and he questioned the prisoners as to why their comrades had pulled out. They said that when we came running at them yelling, hollering and shooting across the open fields, they figured the whole invasion was directed right at them and never dreamed that only twenty men armed with rifles would attack over 200 well-armed soldiers in stone fortifications.

Besides our four dead troopers there was one wounded man and another who sat on a stone floor complaining about his arm hurting. He said it was badly bent, but I could see that it was broken. He said it happened when he hit the ground on the jump but he hadn't found a medic to fix it yet. Tearing the top from a German grenade crate, I fashioned a splint for him and tied it snug from his elbow to his knuckles with strips of parachute canopy. Then I pulled on his fingers until I felt the splintered ends of bone grate past each other. I pulled a little farther so the broken ends would not touch each other, aligned them and tightened down on the strips of silk so the arm would remain in a firm position. After I had his arm in a sling tied around his neck, he thanked me, and I left to look around.

The officers assigned certain areas for each of us to guard, for the Germans were famous for counterattack and we had to have an organized defense against it. Phillips and I had to guard the road leading into town. We picked a spot where a ditch ran from the houses through some trees and connected at right angles with the larger ditch that ran alongside the blacktop road. We could make a good stand from here and if things got too hot, we would stand some chance of making our way back to the fortified houses down the smaller ditch.

We had a case of German grenades, out of some of which we took the handles and wired the heads around a center one with a handle, forming a potato masher with a head the size of a teller mine. If tanks came, we planned to fling these multi-grenades under the tracks and blow them up. It would take two hands to swing them, but we had no bazooka and had to improvise something. Even if we had had just the bazooka rockets, we could have rigged a booby trap for tanks. Almost every trooper, especially the bazooka men, knew how to fix a rocket with wires and a flashlight battery so that it could be launched from its own packing container.

We had, though, gathered all the Hawkins mines from the other troopers and had set them down on the blacktop road. These would cripple a tank, if not stop it altogether. The cattle roamed this district freely and their droppings were scattered on the roads as well as the fields. So we very carefully picked up some cow pies with our hands and flopped them down over the mines to camouflage them. We had just finished when a Frenchman, driving a two-wheeled, one-horse cart approached our newly laid mine field, threatening to destroy himself, his horse and all our hard work. We waved at him trying to stop him, but he just smiled and waved back. When we pointed at the piles of cow manure and exclaimed, "Boom," throwing our hands up in gestures of explosions, he gave us that "Sure buddy, I know" look and started forward again.

Phillips climbed over the edge of the ditch and tried to grab the reins, but the horse reared up and started through the mines. I hit the bottom of the ditch and Phillips came flying head first over the brush that grew alongside the road and landed on top of me. We held our breaths and waited for the explosion that would send that screwball Frenchman and his horse into the next world. At the same time we hugged the ground so we wouldn't get hit by any of the pieces as they made the trip. After a few minutes we slowly raised our heads, peaked over the edge of the ditch, and saw to our surprise that the cart had made it safely through the mine field with the driver sitting jauntily on the seat, oblivious to his near disaster.

The early morning march and the capture of the town had taken only a few hours. It wasn't ten o'clock yet. I felt hungry, having had no breakfast as yet, so Phillips and I each broke open a K ration box marked "breakfast." The chopped pork and egg yolks tasted like a real banquet.

After finishing, we lit cigarettes and leaned against the road bank to enjoy the warm sun. A bullet cracked between us sounding like a .22 rifle as the slug came within inches of our faces. Our reactions were getting faster and we both hit the bottom of the ditch at the same time.

"There he is," yelled Phillips, "I see him. He just ran behind those trees over there and he's heading toward the houses on the right."

We were peeking over the edge again, but I didn't see him right away so we waited and watched the place where we'd last seen him. Then, a little farther to the right, I saw him moving on his hands and knees; or it was another Kraut, but it really didn't matter just as long as it was a Kraut. Easing my rifle up I asked Phillips if he wanted the shot.

"No," he replied, "go ahead."

It was an easy shot, I saw the dust fly from his jacket as I squeezed the trigger and he dropped straight down. There were more out there than the two of us figured on because just then a machine gun opened up and raked the brush around us. As if that were a signal, the whole world seemed to explode in flame, and bullets were flying so thick that it seemed I could reach up and grab a handful out of the air.

All the troopers were firing now, and some of the ones closer to the road were lobbing grenades as far as they could on the other side. It became a pitched battle with only a narrow blacktop road separating the two forces. Actions became automatic, firing at fleeting shapes, crawling to different positions and firing, reloading and firing again and again.

The Germans were in the ditch on one side of the road while we were in the ditch on this side. A distance of not more than fifteen yards separated us. At times, just as I slipped my rifle through the foliage to fire, I could feel the muzzle blasts from the enemy rifles as they fired toward us. The Germans usually dropped back into the ditch while working the bolts of their rifles, but we could nearly always get off one to three shots before ducking back down. We were so close together that our faces were being blackened by the enemy's muzzle blasts. They used a smokeless powder and were hard to locate, whereas our weapons spewed out billows of smoke that gave our positions away and kept us moving to keep from getting our brains blown out. There was very little wind and the smoke hung close around us. The smell of powder burned deep into our nostrils, leaving the backs of our throats and the roofs of our mouths dry, along with a taste like sucking an old copper penny.

The firing died down and soon came to a complete stop as the enemy withdrew, leaving us to count noses again and to close the gaps in our lines left by dead troopers. Things became fairly quiet, with only occasional sniping going on from both sides. Phillips and I lay on the grass watching the artillery drop first in one field then another. The effects of those little white pills were still with us, and we felt calm and a little light-headed as we lay there right after the battle.

"Wonder if that stuff could hurt you?" Phillips asked, as pieces of shell fragments made purring sounds as they arched over our heads. Then without warning several shells landed close by. We saw the ground rise up in a small cloud of black dust, and a cow that had been grazing nearby raised her head as her guts dropped in a pile on the ground. She sank slowly to her front knees, then rolled onto her side and lay still. At the same time several large limbs, one of them as large around as my leg, jumped from the trees around us. We looked at each other and slid back down into the ditch.

"I guess it can," I finally answered as we watched the pool of blood spreading around the carcass of the cow.

From our position we could look down the sloping countryside and view the beach, but there were many wooded, hidden gullies between us and the water that were filled with enemy troops and weapons. Then a battle-ship appeared and slid slowly along parallel with the shore. "That's our Navy," cheered all the men in chorus. "That's our Navy!" The big guns were pointed our way, but we didn't think anything of it until sheets of flame erupted from them and billows of smoke belched out across the water toward the shore. The huge shells sounded like box-cars twisting slowly through the air, coming closer and louder with each turn until they skimmed over the stable where we kept the German prisoners. The tile roof evaporated in red dust as the shells buried themselves in an apple orchard just behind us. The great thump they made burrowing into the ground sent out a shock wave just ahead of the explosion.

Peeking out from under the edge of my helmet, I could see whole apple trees, including dirt free roots, turning end over end high in the air. The prisoners were screaming in mortal terror and Brininstool told them to shut up or he would machine-gun the whole damned bunch. Troopers threw out orange smoke grenades as a signal that friendly troops were in this area, and a great cloud of orange smoke hung over us in the windless air. The ship fired an orange smoke pot in recognition and ceased its fire. We let out a sigh of relief.

"That's the biggest battleship I've ever seen," I told the Lieutenant when he came to check on our position and see if we were still alive. "But why did they fire on us?"

"Well, if you'll look at the map," he said, "you'll find that neither we nor any other friendly troops are supposed to be in this place, and if it hadn't been for the Air Corps fouling up, we wouldn't be here either. But the beach landings should be in by now, and it won't be too long before we get reinforcements and can get on our way to where we are supposed to be."

It was strange in a way. The Germans had a fortress here from which a few men could hold off an army, yet a few men had taken it and now were holding them off even though they outnumbered us almost fifteen to one. Hagenbuch returned from scouting around town and announced that he wanted a volunteer to go with him. He had run into a Kraut in a house while he was looking around, and just as he fired, the German jumped through a window. Hagenbuch jumped out the window after him and chased him down the street. Even though the German was limping from his wound, he reached a church and ran inside just ahead of Hagenbuch. When Hagenbuch entered the building there were about twenty enemy soldiers in there and they opened fire on him.

He leaped back through the door and slammed it shut.

"That's a hell of a thing to do in a church," he grumbled. Now he wanted someone to go back with him and kill those dirty bastards.

A first lieutenant driving a captured French two-man tank volunteered, along with two other troopers. They piled on top of the tank, the lieutenant gunned the engine and they roared down the road, with Hagenbuch pointing the way. An hour later the tank returned with Hagenbuch lying facedown on the deck, he had just been stunned, but the other two troopers had been killed and the officer had a bullet in his neck. The bullet had passed almost all the way through from the right side to the left and was lying pretty close to the surface, forming a big lump. He brought the tank to a stop and said he didn't feel good, so we helped him from the tank and placed him on the grass under the trees. The other troopers said I had done a good job setting the arm earlier, so they elected me to remove the bullet. I didn't want the job but someone had to do it.

After building a fire from one of the German packing crates, I heated my trench knife while another trooper gave the officer a shot of morphine. He was cold and clammy-feeling, and his tan skin had suddenly taken on a pallor that looked kind of sickly, but he did not pass out, even when I cut in his neck. The bullet did not come out easily and when the ordeal was finally over, he looked up at me and said in a weak voice, "I don't think I'm going to make it."

It was the first thing he had said. All through the operation he hadn't even groaned. We covered him as best we could to keep him warm against shock. The last time I saw him he was still living and looked as though he was getting better.

The rest of the day passed easily and we consolidated our positions while we talked about the beach landings and how long it would be before friendly troops reached us. I started piling cobblestones across the end of the ditch. Phillips joined in and we built a wall about two feet high across the end of the ditch where it connected at right angles to the road. Night came and several men crawled into the ditch behind Phillips and me to give support in case tanks tried to come into town on the road. Earlier we had taken extra precautions against tanks by blowing trees across the road in a crisscross pattern with prima cord and blocks of TNT.

Just when night was at its darkest a shadow appeared above us and started spraying up and down the ditch with a burp gun. He was a big man and stood with feet wide apart, like he owned the whole damned world. There was nothing we could do but lie flat in the ditch for the brief seconds it took him to empty his magazine. While he was snapping another in place some of the men fired at him and he started to run. I threw a grenade, yelling, "Fire in the hole." We ducked, and as soon as it went off the shooting really started hot and heavy. One Kraut, evidently knowing this place well, crept up to the other side of the road, lined himself up with the ditch we were in and opened fire with a burp gun. Phillips lobbed a grenade in his direction. The firing stopped with the blast. Not one of the machine pistol's bullets got past the stones we had piled at the open end of the ditch. Fifteen minutes' work had saved our asses.

Grenades were bouncing like popcorn in a hopper, with small arms fire going back and forth at a fast rate for a few minutes. The firing gradually slowed, the Germans pulled out and the firing quit altogether. Again we took roll call; our ranks were getting pretty thin by now. Phillips called out to see if anyone was hurt and crawled back down the ditch but everyone seemed to be O.K. Then we spotted Justo (pronounced Hoo Sto) sitting on the edge of the bank holding his helmet on his head and gently rocking back and forth groaning under his breath. We asked him if he was hit. He said no but wouldn't look up at us. It was then we noticed the hole in the front of his helmet and the one coming out the back. It took two men to get his helmet off, what with him holding it on. But finally it came off, and he reached up with his forefinger, trembling a little, and gently tapped his forehead, half expecting to find a hole there. The bullet had entered the front of his helmet, spun around between the steel and liner and tore out the back leaving Justo with nothing more than a headache.

"I thought the whole top of my head was gone!" he exclaimed with relief, and flashed about three yards of white teeth in a wide grin. "Man," he said, "if I live through this and get back to Texas, all I'm going to do is make violent love to my girlfriend."

"Baloney," I said, "you don't know how to make violent love."

"Come along and watch me sometime, violent love, Mexican style," he replied.

It was just a damned miracle, as close as we were together in that ditch and having a whole magazine of ammo sprayed through us like water from a garden hose, that the only casualty was Justo's helmet.

There were some rumors going around that the beach landings had been repulsed and that we were stranded here to fight it out the best we could. The rest of the night passed pretty quietly and just before the first cold light of dawn, we saw a sight that I will never forget—American infantry coming up the hill through the hedgerows. Glider boots, canvas leggings worn by the infantry and glidermen, never looked so good before. So passed our first day and two nights of combat. It wouldn't be too long before the sun would be coming up, a full bright red, on June 7, 1944. Lieutenant Muir hobbled to the road using a stick for a cane and called us together to take roll call. There were ten of us from the 101st and a lieutenant and two men from the 82nd, thirteen men left out of the original twenty-two. Twenty-two men counting Nick and Archie who were not in the actual assault on Ravenoville. There were other dead and wounded troops in town. They had gotten it taking the first half of town before we got there.

We hadn't done badly though. We had dispersed over 200 enemy troops, captured a fortified town, taken seventy-five prisoners, killed at least that many more and now commanded the high ground overlooking this portion of Utah beach.

"Well, now that friendly troops have taken over," the Lieutenant said, "we can leave this place and head for our original objectives."

The officer of the 82nd said he would take his men and head out because he had to be in Ste. Mère-Église and the whole operation depended on the Airborne completing their individual missions.

Several of us walked back through town to see if we had missed anything. Coming to the house where the four troopers had been machine-gunned, we saw a jeep that had come in from the beach landing. The jeep was parked by the gate leading into the weed-choked front yard. A man holding a camera asked us to walk through the yard past our dead while he stood in the door of the house and took our picture.

"You go to hell," I said. "I'm not going to pose over any of my dead buddies."

"The people back home need to know what's going on," he said. "Besides, you may want the picture later."

Still I refused, but some of the other troopers moved through the yard with weapons at ready and he got his picture.

We returned to Lieutenant Muir, wished the 82nd men good luck and started on our way. We hadn't gone fifty yards when there was a roaring of an engine and we dove for the ditches as a German half track came plowing around the bend. We waited for it to hit the mines that were still scattered on the road, but then we noticed the orange marker panels tied to the front and the sides. One of our men jumped up and yelled for them to stop, pointing at the mines still covered with cow dung. The driver hit the brakes and swerved just in time to keep from hitting them. The troopers came tumbling out of the half track laughing and joking like a bunch of baggy pants clowns. They held their weapons in anything but a military manner and brandished jugs of wine and cognac. A broad-shouldered, narrow-waisted private swaggered toward us and asked how we liked his private limousine. He looked a little hurt when Lieutenant Muir told him that it would make too good a target for either our tanks or the Germans' and that he would have to leave it here.

These men had assembled much as we had during the night. Trying to orient themselves in the morning they had stumbled onto a German fortification, had attacked it and come away with the spoils. Now they were trying to make it to their objectives on time. Up to now they had seen no other friendly troops. There were no officers among them, not even a noncom. It was a good feeling to know that all the Airborne forces had been so thoroughly briefed on this invasion that once oriented, each and every man, without the aid of map or compass, could find his way to his assigned objective. The new men passed the bottles around and we all drank heavily and munched K rations. Men from both divisions were in the new group, so part of them went with the other officer and four or five of them joined us.

With scouts out and Lieutenant Muir in command we started out in the direction of St. Côme-du-Mont. Just before we got to the crossroads two machine guns opened up and small arms fire raked us. But luck was still with us and no one was hit. Everyone scrambled for the safety of houses and foxholes. The Krauts had the road out of town blocked. Several times different troopers tried to break through, but each time were driven back under a withering hail of fire. Finally Red Knight and Brininstool routed the prisoners out of the stables, lined them up on the road in a column of two's and, counting cadence, marched them down the hill toward the machine guns. They were hoping the enemy wouldn't fire on their own, but it didn't make any difference to the men on the machine guns, and they opened up, drilling holes in their own comrades in trying to hit the American troopers. The prisoners started screaming, "Nicht schiessen" (don't shoot), and leaped headfirst for the ditch, and possible escape, so we opened up on them too. The poor bastards were caught in a murderous cross fire, and before the shooting stopped they were all dead.

One of the new troopers who had arrived on the half track dropped his rifle and with a war whoop ran straight at the machine-gun closest to the intersection. His action probably unnerved the gunner because, although he fired a steady string at the oncoming trooper, he never did touch him. In just a few seconds he covered the distance, leaped over the gun and slashed the German's throat from ear to ear with his trench knife. Then, with a quick left jab, he knocked the other Kraut backward and plunged the knife through his belt up to the hilt. With both of these Krauts dead the men on the other gun tried to make a break, but were shot down before they could run a dozen steps. With the road open we re-formed and started our long trek again, kidding the knife-wielding trooper that he had been eating too many of those little white pills.

The Lieutenant was limping pretty badly now, so we stopped for a break. He was having a hard time keeping up. After resting a few minutes, he gave the order to move out again, but when he tried to get up he just couldn't make it. He told me that a grenade had landed in his foxhole during the night's fighting and blown up between the dirt wall and the gas mask tied to his leg. Although his flesh hadn't been torn, there was a large bruise and the bone had been fractured. He had thought he could keep up with us anyway, but now knew he would have to fall out because he could feel the ends of the bone grating together. We had to leave him behind to make his own way back to town as well as possible, and the rest of us, all privates, to get to St. Côme-du-Mont as soon as we could. No one was in command at this time. We just knew we had to be at a certain place at a certain time. So we fell into combat formation and started out.

On the march we passed through a section that had been blasted to rubble. I don't know whether it was from bombing or shelling from one of the large battleships. The trees were shredded stumps with wisps of smoke or ground fog laced through them. The ground was plowed into loose dirt with large craters scattered all over. The whole scene reminded me of some oil paintings I had seen from time to time that were reputed to have been painted by some demented artist. Not a single bird flew in the area, nor did I see an insect on the ground. A deathly silence hung over the place like a suffocating blanket.

The shuffling sound of our boots, along with an occasional pebble being kicked across the hard surface of the blacktop, sounded loud. I thought to myself that this must be the home of death itself.

We kept walking and soon left the desolate place behind. The fields on either side of the road became greener and more peaceful as we moved along. The sun was up now and the air warmer. A French woman was standing on the shoulder of the road with a two wheeled cart. As we came alongside of her Phillips asked what was in the cans on the cart. She opened one can and we saw that it was filled with milk, real fresh milk, something we rarely saw in the Paratroops. Phillips pulled out his canteen cup and asked her to fill it.

"Don't take her milk," I said. "These people don't have too much to eat now."

"Neither do I," Phillips replied. "We've got a lot to do and I'm not going to do it on an empty stomach if I can help it."

That sounded like a good argument, so I held my canteen cup out too. She filled both of them without a smile. I gave her a pack of cigarettes. She took them, put them in her smock and stood staring at us without any facial expression whatsoever. We finished the milk while walking in column with the other troopers.

On we went, passing through Foucarville, St. Germain-de-Varreville and St. Martin-de-Varreville, sometimes being fired on by enemy small arms and sometimes getting hit pretty heavy. Audoville-la-Hubert fell behind us, then a small cluster of houses with no town name. At Herbert we made a right turn and headed through a place that had swamps on either side of the road. It reminded me a lot of some of the places I used to hunt back in Michigan. It surprised all of us to see a Sherman tank bogged down in the swamp to the left because we didn't think the beach landings had gotten in this far yet. Thinking back on it, the tanks had every right to be there, for the road running through Herbert was actually exit 2, running from the Utah beach clear to St. Côme-du-Mont. Then we saw three burned-out American tanks and one still smoking German tank to the left and farther ahead.

"That's not very good odds," Phillips said. "I hope we have enough Shermans to last through the war."

Gunfire sounded from up ahead and we could make out the tall spire of a church which marked the center of a town.

"Here we go again," Justo said with a look of disgust. "How come they haven't got this town taken yet? Guess we'll have to do it for them."

"Like hell," a big private replied. "We've got other things to do; so when we get to that town everybody keeps moving, understand?"

Just before we reached the town the big private shouted double-time and we automatically picked up cadence and started jogging at a pace that we were all so familiar with. We passed a road sign marked Ste. Marie-du-Mont and saw troopers crouched in doorways and lying in gutters along the road. Firing was coming in from the other end of the street as well as going out from this end, but we kept on with a steady rhythmic running until one of the troopers yelled to us that all of the town wasn't taken yet.

"Hell, we know that," one of the men up front replied, "but we've got other things to do right now."

The Krauts opened fire on us and we returned fire, shooting from the hip as we ran, but didn't hit any of them as far as I could see. A trooper, about the third one in front of me, went down and rolled into the ditch on the left and I could see as I ran past that he was dead. Just a lucky hit, but one of our men was gone. We kept the same cadence and ran on right through the town. On the outskirts we came on several American troopers sprawled dead along the roadside, and although we didn't stop to examine them closely, I did see that they were all lying face up. Then the weak feeling came back in my stomach and for the first time I wished I were somewhere else. For they had their pants pulled down and their manhood had either been shot or cut completely away, leaving nothing but blood-caked, gaping wounds in their crotches. The way they were lying, shoulder to shoulder, made this look like anything but an act of war.

Once clear of the village we had pretty good going until we ran into some troopers who had teamed up with two Sherman tanks and were mopping up some Germans in the fields on either side of the road. We joined with them in firing on the enemy in the ditches ahead, but they were too well dug in to get hit with rifle fire. The turret on one of the tanks opened and the tank commander said that he would flush them out for us. He maneuvered his tank so that one tread was on the road and the other in the ditch, then started moving forward at a walking pace. When he reached the enemy several of them tried running out across the fields and road but were cut down by our rifle fire. Three of those who stayed in the ditch were crushed under the track of the tank. They screamed so loud and shrilly that I thought for sure their lungs were ruptured and their throats shredded before they died. This was too much for the rest of them, and they all flushed at once, half heading across the field and half across the road. None of them made it.

The way was clear now and we started out once more and went right to the outskirts of Vierville. Men were lined head to toe in the ditches and a noncom yelled for us to get down, that the enemy mortars had this place zeroed in and were raising hell with troops up and down the road. One man was dead in the ditch and another lay on his back in the middle of the road. There was nothing any one could do but feel sorry for him. He lay there staring with unblinking eyes at the clear bue sky, while his throat moved as though he were trying to breathe but just couldn't get the air into his lungs. Every few minutes his belly would suck deep up into his chest, stay that way for a moment, then return to a relaxed position. I watched him for a while and thought to myself that this was a hell of a way to die, he just didn't want to give up the ghost.

Word passed back down the line to get ready for an attack on the town. We would jump off on command from the head of the column. While lying there, Phillips, Justo, Bernie and myself talked to the other men who had already been fighting for possession of this town. They had had a pretty rough time of it. It seems that the town had been taken once by elements of the 506, who had slammed on through and headed for Beaumont, much as we had taken, then left, Ravenoville. Enemy troops had counterattacked from the sides after the first 506 units had passed through and were now pouring fire at us from the fortified houses. Small arms fire got heavier and heavier, shouting reached us, men who were scattered through the fields on our right started running forward. Men in the ditches ahead of us rose up, looked over their shoulders, yelled, "Let's go," and waved us on as they started forward.

The attack snowballed. Soon troopers were everywhere,

all heading for the buildings ahead. I didn't recognize anyone. Phillips and Brininstool weren't anywhere in sight. I
didn't attach myself to any one squad, but went along with
what seemed to be the largest flow of troopers. Gaining
the town, we worked our way to the left, toward the
hedges, to take up positions against another counterattack.
Large groups of German prisoners were being herded onto
the main road and back the way we had come. A colonel
with a .45 in his hand ran into the hedge-surrounded field
we were in and started barking orders. The most I could
get from them was that we weren't finished yet, but had to
keep going through the next town. We were deployed with
other men far out to the left flank. The fields here seemed
larger, the sun was shining brightly, and I was tired. Even
with all the firing going on I still felt I could immediately
go to sleep in the warm sun.

Again men shouted and started forward, and although I
wasn't sure which way was forward anymore, I went along
with them, shouting, yelling and crashing through hedges.
In field after field we were fired on by burp guns and
slammed by mortar fire, but we could not make physical
contact with the Krauts. We fired into the hedges where
we thought they would be as we ran. The enemy lay in the
heavy hedges firing at us as we charged them. Then they
faded away to rear positions as we neared the hedge they
were firing from, leaving behind only their dead. Heavy
fire fighting sounded to our right in the direction of a town
which I found out later was Angoville-au-Plain. Artillery
moaned far overhead, and from the sounds, they were
large shells, heading deep into enemy territory.

We had traveled for what seemed to be miles, through

thickets, hedges and fields, until finally we came on a large group of men deployed in skirmish lines facing another town. These men weren't moving, just spread out in the open as though waiting for something to happen. The men I was with melted into their lines as though they belonged. I lay next to a sergeant who asked me what outfit I was with and seemed sort of surprised when I told him A Company 506. To our right two officers, one with a radio, were talking and studying a map. The noncom said the officer with the radio was a forward observer for the Navy.

"What the hell is the Navy doing here?" I asked.

"He took special training and parachuted in with us," answered the sergeant.

"On its way," the man with the radio said aloud. "One, two, three, four," he counted as the sound of big shells came closer.

"Now," the observer said, and at that moment the shells started exploding in German-held land. He studied the map, watched the shellbursts for a little while, then radioed corrections. Again he started to count, keeping rhythmic time with pointed index finger. The finger came down hard. "Now," he said, as the shells hit. A lone two-story brick house had been standing quite a ways in front of us and a little to our right. Now it was nothing but a pile of rubble. The accuracy of that artillery was frightening.

The barrage continued for what seemed to be about a half hour, working the hedges and enemy emplacements. Some of it landed in our own lines, killing several men, wounding others. Some of the men moved from the line of shellfire and ran to better positions. Then the shelling lifted and again we attacked. Swinging to our right, crossing hedges and fields, we came onto a blacktop road, then turned left and went into town under heavy fire. The enemy counterattacked with their infantry and by sheer numbers they forced us out. But we slammed back with ferocity and gained part of the town. Next came their famed SS, which forced us to withdraw. But the troopers recovered quickly and again retook half the town.

Then came a real shock. Horse-mounted cavalry charged in, and after bitter fighting the town was again in enemy hands. We found out from a few prisoners taken in the withdrawal that the horse cavalry was made up of White Russians who had sided with the Germans. The roads, fields and town were littered with dead from both sides. We lay in the ditches and hedges, hot, tired, dirty, sweaty and thirsty. I had been rationing the water in my canteen, but it was still almost empty now. Water, how important water is to men in combat. What I wouldn't have given then for one quart of cold, clear, sparkling water.

Then the order came and we were in another wild charging melee, yelling at the top of our lungs, cursing and fighting. Glancing to the right I could see other troopers scattered through the fields and making their way over the hedgerow which grew close to the edge of town. On we went into town, running down the street and straight into the heavy fire of the enemy. Then we were amongst them, and door to door fighting started in house by deadly house, room by deadly room.

We shot and grenaded our way through the houses and streets. Entering one house on the run I found myself in a room. A stairway on the right led to a second floor, a door on my left opened to another larger room. I swung into the room on the left just as a medic entered the house behind me. I caught a glimpse of his long red handlebar mustache as he flipped a long-barreled six-shooter up from the hip and blasted at the top of the stairs. A Kraut with a burp gun came tumbling down in a heap. The German must have just started down the stairs when I entered the room on the left and the medic came in the door. Just before I left the house I wondered, "where in the hell did he get that cowboy six-gun?"

When we finally had time to breathe it was on the far side of town. The remnants of the White Russian horse cavalry had withdrawn to the surrounding fields and hedgerows and were regrouping with the shards of German infantry and once proud SS. Horses wandered aimlessly in the streets or grazed in the fields, for they no longer had masters to ride them. We were in a ditch on a side road just off the main drag of town trying to eat some K rations and gnaw on the dog biscuits that come with them when some screwball officer, a colonel, carrying a .45 automatic in his right hand and pacing back and forth on the road, started barking orders in a loud voice. I don't know who he was, but he should have been someplace else, for he gave an order for us to line up in a column of two's and get ready to move out. We openly protested, but he insisted that it was an order and we reluctantly lined up on the blacktop in perfect target column of two's and waited for the order to move out.

I found myself standing next to Phillips. How and when we met up again is still a mystery to me. Looking around, I could see a lot of other men from A Company too. Where had they all come from? Had I joined them or had they joined the bunch I was with? I don't know how it happened, but here were a lot of men from my company and we were talking as though we had never been separated. If they weren't going to mention it, neither would I. I didn't want them to think I was going nuts. A lot of other troopers from the regiment were here now also, and buddies who hadn't seen each other since boarding the planes in England were congratulating each other on still being alive. But some friends were dead or wounded and some were still trying to make it to their assigned objectives from far-off places where the Air Corps had scattered them.

The road on which we stood had banks about six feet high on either side. Two German prisoners stood next to the one on our left as we faced the main street. We were going to leave them behind to be guarded by our walking wounded. Suddenly it seemed as if every machine gun this side of hell opened up and ripped long strings of bullets in crisscross patterns through our ranks. Men dove headfirst for the ditches, and Phillips and I landed side by side in the bottom of the one on our right. I rolled on my right shoulder and came up to the rim of the ditch and saw troopers writhing on the road in their death throes. These were the unlucky ones who just happened to get it. The colonel with the .45 was nowhere in sight. The two German prisoners tried to climb the steep bank behind them, but just as they got to the top, Brininstool fired his tommy gun. Both of them slid down, whirled around and were slammed back against the bank so hard by the .45 slugs that their eyes popped out of their sockets and hung down on their cheeks. What kept them standing is a mystery to me, but neither one fell. They just stood in a leaning position, side by side against the dirt wall, with arms hanging loosely at their sides. From the expression on their faces they must have just looked through the open gates of hell.

With the Wehrmacht, SS and the Russian cavalry beaten in turn out of town, that one officer had thought we had the world by the ass and had lined us up on the road with our guard down. We never did see the enemy paratroopers who crawled within fifty feet of us and now were doing everything in their power to destroy us. Very few privates have ever been to college, none to O.C.S., but every private there had more sense, combat sense, than that colonel. We all knew what was going to happen and had argued against his order. But he had the authority.

We were firing blindly in the direction of the sounds of enemy weapons. They were well hidden and blasting at us with every automatic weapon they had at their disposal. Smoke filled the air, burned powder almost choked us, and as we were caught by surprise, confusion reigned.

Suddenly shouts of "Let's go" sounded above the holocaust. Looking out of the ditch I saw fast moving figures in light tan jump suits with large baggy pockets racing crouched over through the heavy gunfire in the direction of the enemy. Men weren't waiting for orders or commands, just busting out and running head-on at the dirty bastards who were blasting at us from two directions with automatic weapons. The fever spread and more and more men left the ditches and within seconds we were all up and charging in a wild mob toward an enemy that we wanted to crush and kill. Just as I cleared the road I glanced to the left and saw the two dead Germans still standing with their eyes hanging on their cheeks, and somehow the image of them burned into my mind. Even now if I stop and think about them, they rise up to stand side by side against the dirt wall.

Phillips and I cleared the bank on the opposite side of the road, and along with the masses of other troopers, we went storming across the fields and took the enemy by a hell of a surprise. They expected us to fall back under their pointblank fire, but instead we ran headlong into it and turned the attack onto them. Running across the fields I came upon a young German man paratrooper lying belly down and firing a burp gun in our general direction. As he saw me his eyes became round and wide with fear. He rolled onto his right side, swinging his weapon with the same movement and squirting a long string of fire. The bullets crackled past my ears just as I shot him through the head. His comrade just to his right started to roll over and over in the grass in an attempt to get away, but another trooper laced him through the ribs with a tommy gun.

Some of the troopers were turning to the right and making their way across the main drag, so the rest of us followed, figuring the main body of Krauts was in that direction. Somehow Phillips and I got separated again in the scramble, and I joined three other men carrying an air-cooled machine gun. They were Trotter, Barrington and Hundley carrying the machine gun on a tripod with half a belt of ammo wrapped loosely around the barrel and ready to fire. All of them carried boxes of ammo at the same time, so my offer to help carry the load was taken right

away. Barrington took the front of the gun and with
Hundley carrying the back two legs and Trotter and I
loaded with ammo we started out across hedgerows into
enemy country. Brush grew so thick around the edge of
the fields, that in crawling through it and over the hedges,
we soon found that the four of us were crossing a field with
no sign of any other troopers around. Firing was going on
all around us and we were hot, sweaty and tired. We had
run until I thought we were all going to drop.

A machine gun blasted at us from our right flank in a
long ripping burp typical of German machine guns, showering us with hot lead. We dropped right where we were,
as though we were dead. The Kraut blasted at us again and
I could hear the bullets slamming into the ground around
us. Then Trotter jumped up and ran the last few steps to a
hedgerow and disappeared into a hole. He yelled for us to
join him and Hundley and I leaped head first into the hole
after him, but Barrington lay where he fell. We lay there
waiting for them to attack, but nothing happened and we
could see nothing in the underbrush to shoot at. Trotter
took the lead again and stepped boldly into the open. He
had a lot of guts to step out like that in front of a hidden
machine gun and walk around in the middle of the field
trying to draw fire on himself. It must have been a lone
Kraut who fired on us, then took off, because there were
no more shots.

Hundley and I crawled out and dragged Barrington into
the protection of the hole and found that he was still alive
and conscious. He had a bullet hole in his left forearm.
Trotter and I stood guard while Hundley bandaged the

arm and Barrington told us that he had played dead, hoping the Kraut wouldn't fire again. We propped him up in the hole, gave him his rifle and told him to stay there. Taking the ammo he had been carrying and with Hundley on the front of the gun and me on the back, we started out on the double to catch up with the rest of our men, whom we thought now far in advance.

We passed field after field, hedgerow after hedgerow in our run to catch up. We ran until our lungs seemed to be on fire and my windpipe felt raw and ragged, as though someone had poured hot sand down it. But still we could not see any sign of our comrades. It got to the point where I wanted to find a place to hole up and catch our breath. Suddenly we came to a place from which we could look down a long sloping landscape and see a broad river. But still no sign of any of our troops. As we stood there wondering what to do next, two other men emerged from a hedge to our left rear. They turned out to be Chute Johnson and Hagenbuch. They told us they were lost. But that wasn't anything new to us. So were we. Then we saw Germans running from the same direction we had just come from. But they turned and started crossing the road on our right without seeing us standing at the far end of the field. Our group and theirs must have been running almost side by side, with only a hedge separating us.

The road here headed toward the river and gradually tapered downward, but the hedgerows and fields on either side remained quite a bit higher, so that the closer the road got to the river, the higher the banks were alongside it. At the point where we now stood the bank was about eight or ten feet high. The German troops were sliding down it, running across the road and climbing the bank at the other side. Hagenbuch was all for going after them and called to Hundley and me to bring the machine gun down onto the road where we could get clear shooting at them. Hagenbuch was dark haired, younger and smaller than me and always laughing. Even now he had a smile on his face. The little guy sure had guts. Some of his nerve must have rubbed off on me, for when he slid down the road bank I was right behind him with the machine gun. Down on the road I opened up with the gun while Trotter, Chute and Hundley started firing with rifles.

The enemy was taken completely by surprise but recovered quickly and returned fire. At the same time some of their comrades started firing from the other side of the road. There were men over there we didn't know about. Two belts of ammo were burned through the gun. Someone threw another can down the bank to us which Hagenbuch loaded in the gun and I continued to fire at the remaining Krauts who were still trying to get up the dirt bank for the protection of the other side of the hedge. My fire was slashing through them. Some of them fell back to the blacktop and the ditch. Two enemy machine guns now opened up from the other hedgerow. Bullets skipped along the blacktop like flat stones being skipped across a mill pond, but sparking each time they hit. Others snapped at our cheeks as they ripped past our heads. I didn't see how they could miss, for we were in the middle of the road without cover or concealment.

There was another long burst from the enemy and my machine gun jerked violently as bullets tore through the tripod and barrel jacket. Strings of bullets tearing past our heads made their familiar crackling sounds, but at the same time I heard a "plock" like sound, and Hagenbuch jerked backward, then fell face forward. A bullet had passed through the top of his head killing him. Two bullets had passed through the barrel jacket and three through the tripod. It was time to get the gun to the other side of the hedgerow to make a stand from a more protected place.

Cradling the forty-two-pound machine gun in my arms, I crawled up the bank and rolled over the top to safety on the other side. Firing was going on hot and heavy now and Trotter was running up and down the length of the field, firing from different places through the brush to give the Krauts the impression that there were more troops on this side than there really were. He ran up to me and asked if I had any grenades. I gave him three of mine. He took off with them and the machine gun, back toward the corner where we first saw the enemy troops crossing the road.

I can't explain the reason, but every time I had the chance to stop I felt an overwhelming drowsiness, the urge to fall asleep. We had been virtually without sleep since June 3rd, but we had been without sleep before on maneuvers. I think the reason had more to do with the mental than the physical strain we were under. Even now I felt very tired and rolled over on my back, lit a cigarette and listened as the incoming fire got heavier and heavier, until it seemed as if there were a solid sheet of lead overhead. Brush and limbs were being chopped from the hedges as bullets raked the top and thudded into the other side. Trotter came running back down the line and told me to get busy, the war was still on and there were still plenty of Krauts out there. Trotter was from Montana, stood about

five feet ten and weighed about 170 pounds. His eyes were
narrow slits in a round face that reminded me of a huge
bull dog. For all his stocky appearance the man was fast,
fast reaction and fast moving. He didn't hang around to see
what I was going to do. He was too busy giving the Krauts
a hard time.

Easing my head back up to the top, I could see the
leaves jumping on the other side from muzzle blasts and
fired on them as fast and as accurately as I could, squeez-
ing each shot with careful deliberation. An 88 shell exploded in the bank on our side of the road and the war
suddenly became lopsided against us. An 88 shell travels
faster than a rifle bullet, so when it's fired point-blank, a
man can't hear it coming until after it explodes, when it's
too late. The big gun slammed at us repeatedly, working
the hedges and fields with methodic deadliness. The exploding shells and the booming report of the cannon
sounded above the small arms fire. Then, to add to our
troubles, a German mortar off to our left flank started
dropping H.E. shells around us, making us seek out the
low spots in the ground. Fragments from these shells scud-
ded along from an inch to several feet above the ground,
cutting the grass and everything else that got in their way
like miniature scythes.

Trotter had more guts than any man should have, for
while the rest of us fired from our positions, he kept running back and forth through this deadly hail of fire, firing
at the enemy and chucking grenades over the road at different intervals. I could see his sweat-streaked, dirty face
as he ran past me. Little beads of grime necklaced the lines
of his neck. He showed no fear, just a great big mad on for

the enemy. Jumping up, I followed him to the left end of the field where we both fell in behind a hedge and tried to spot the mortar. But we could see no sign of it. A few minutes later the mortar became silent and Trotter headed back down the line leaving me to cover the left flank. Lying there watching for the men who were manning the gun, I became aware of a hell of a lot of shooting coming from our rear and realized that it was our own troops fighting their way in our direction. We were better than half a mile in front of our own lines.

It's no wonder the German troops hadn't seen us when they were crossing the road. They never expected to find Americans this far behind their own lines and they were probably pulling back to form another main line of resistance when we intercepted them. Our happening to be here sure put the skids under their plans and now we had to stick it out until friendly troops arrived. Then the thought came to mind that when our troops did arrive, we would be caught in a small area and a heavy cross fire from both sides. But we would worry about that when the time came.

The sun felt warm and good, and I became relaxed even with the heavy fire going on until a figure came out of the brush about a hundred yards out, just about where the mortar should have been. He quickly disappeared into another clump of brush before I could draw proper bead on him. Swinging the rifle to the right and taking a bead on the far end of the brush, I waited until he stepped out and walked across a small opening at the edge of a crumbled brick farmhouse. "They must be out of shells and this man is going for a new supply," I thought, as I squeezed the trigger. He went down hard and rolled over on a small pile of bricks, then, lying on his back, he dug his heels into the ground and twitched for several minutes. Finally, taking a deep breath, he arched his back up until only his shoulders and heels were touching the ground, then collapsed. I could have put another bullet into him, but somehow I was fascinated and watched him in his losing battle for life. As soon as it ended, I poured round after round in the spot where the mortar was hidden.

Lying there in the warm sun guarding our left flank I watched the shrubbery and bushes for any movement or sign of life that would give an enemy's position away—a moving shadow, a puff of smoke from a cigarette or a small cloud of dust drifting on the breeze from behind a bush— anything at all that would help me locate and destroy another enemy. Every once in a while I would glance at the dead man, and I suddenly noticed his long blond hair. GIs were never allowed to have hair that long, and it agitated me in a strange way that I can't explain. Deep inside, something primitive stirred within me, and I thought of the muskrats and other game I had skinned for their pelts. Then the whole thing became clear to me. I wanted that scalp.

Nerves quivered throughout the entire length of my body and my hands became cold and sweaty as I slid over the top of the hedge and started crawling toward him. Thoughts of how I would salt and stretch the scalp on a small willow limb filled my mind. I could carry it inside my shirt. And how nice it would look hanging on my living- room wall after the war was over. The prize was nearly within my reach when rifle fire opened up on me, and I was forced to run like hell and dive behind the safety of the hedgerow. Two more times I tried to reach him, but each time was driven back by stubborn squareheads trying to punch 8 mm holes in my skin. Finally I decided to forget the whole damned thing and concentrate on business at hand and leave the trophies to someone else.

The high whining of a powerful engine came to our ears and I could hear Hundley yell, "The dirty bastards are sending tanks against us. It isn't enough that they've got us outnumbered and got artillery and mortars but now the yellow bastards are trying to get at us with tanks."

The noise became louder and we could hear the clanking of the treads as the metal monster walked toward us. The brush on a low spot in a hedge behind us thrashed wildly for an instant, then gave way, and out lumbered a small General Grant tank mounted with a 37 mm cannon. It was one of ours. We all waved at it. The tank commander stuck his head out of the turret and directed the tank toward us. After briefing him on our situation he joined in with the deception and speeded his tank up and down the hedge, firing with machine gun and cannon from different spots as he went to give the impression that there were several tanks instead of just one.

The pitched battle was still going on. With more coming in than going out we realized that the five of us were fighting a force far greater than we dared imagine. Finally the tanker stopped and told us that he was out of ammo and he would have to go back for more, but would tell the others of our situation and return when he had a refill of ammo. I hated to see the tank leave even if it was out of ammo. It gave us all a feeling of security just to have it with us.

"Hurry up," I told him, "and for God's sake, don't forget us."

"I won't forget you," he answered, and without buttoning up the tank, started out.

Turning around he headed to the right end of the field, then, instead of cutting back the way he had come, through the hedges, he turned onto the road so he could make better time. That was a mistake. For when he came into view of the 88 near the corner, they drilled an armor-piercing shell clear through the turret. The small tank erupted in a violent explosion and started to burn. The whole crew died instantly. We could smell their flesh cooking in the flames, along with the heavy oily smoke. Seeing the tank crew die that way made me feel bad. That commander was a hell of a nice guy.

At that moment other paratroopers started pouring through the hedges from behind us and from the right flank and we knew we had it made now. Turning around we yelled, "Hubba-hubba one time," and waved them on. The first ones that reached us we bitched at for taking so long and asked what the hell kept them. They were men of D Company. They told us the Krauts were on the run and we had better keep them that way so they wouldn't have a chance to dig in. But the fire power from the other side of the road was still coming in so heavy that the men of D Company were obliged to take cover with us. More troopers kept piling in behind us.

A forward observer for the artillery came up, took in the situation and began relaying information and grid coordinates to the batteries in the rear. After a few minutes he murmured under his breath, "On its way." Within moments, shells came screaming in overhead, slamming deep into Kraut lines. He radioed back a few corrections and told them to "Give it hell." There was a constant bridgework of shells shrieking and screaming in, grinding life, limb and equipment to shreds. Incoming fire faded away, our artillery lifted and the enemy seemed only too glad to let things stand that way and be quiet for a while.

More men from A Company followed D Company to our positions. We formed together and dug in for the night. Later that night someone told us we would have to rejoin the rest of the outfit back in Beaumont. Moving out through the night in a group we finally arrived back in Beaumont and dug in next to an American tank that was still burning. Early the next morning, before the sun came up, we were up and formed, ready for another attack. Moving in low along the hedges through dew-soaked grass, we formed a line of skirmishers facing the same enemy-held ground that we had faced the evening before.

Another artillery observer moved up with us and taking his position at a hedge, gave coordinates over the radio. Soon the shells were landing hard on enemy emplacements. The Krauts had an effective weapon in the 88 but the amount of shells our side could throw, along with its accuracy and delicate time fire, made me glad that I was on this side and not the other. Farther to our left the small tank that had been hit the day before still smoked a little. The body of the tank commander who had been so nice to us still sat in the turret. It stayed sitting in the turret for several days. Men started referring to the spot as "the corner where the dead man's in the tank." Later this became known as "Dead Man's Corner," and is still known by this name in France today.

The barrage lifted and we were heading across field after field, screaming and yelling in wild charges that drove the enemy back toward the river. Just before we reached it, they put in a last desperate bid to hold the ground on this side. Again artillery was called in, and it did the heavy work while we took care of the hand-to-hand part. Down next to the river the last ones we ran into were a large group of Hungarians who fought until their capture or death was imminent. Then they came stumbling and crawling out of the hedges with tears streaming down their cheeks, crying like babies and begging us not to shoot them. Their cries of "Nicht schiessen, me Hoongarry" could be heard all up and down the hedges. They were a sickening bunch.

The fight had lasted most of the day. It was afternoon now. We had taken the city of St. Côme-du-Mont and all the high ground surrounding it. We re-formed our units and dug in on a static line of defense on the high ground overlooking the river. Two troopers had one of the 88s that had been firing on us and along with two German prisoners turned it around and pointed it toward Carentan across the river. It was a large field type with oversized casings that had to be loaded after the projectile. While digging my foxhole I casually watched the troopers. It didn't dawn on me what they were doing, but they took a shell casing, filled it with small powder bags and tried to fit the projectile in the end of it. The casing was so full that they pulled some of the powder bags out and finally got the whole works in the breech of the big gun.

Whether the German prisoners knew what was going to happen or not I don't know, but they gave no sign of it. Suddenly one of the troopers yelled, "Now, Hitler, count your children," and pulled the lanyard. There was a hell of an explosion and when the smoke cleared a portion of the blacktop road was torn up and the whole rear of the gun was destroyed. The barrel lay on the ground and the four men had disappeared, except for one German leg with the boot still on it. They never knew what hit them.

Again Phillips and I had paired up and now we leaned on the edge of our foxholes eating K rations and enjoying the view of the river. We watched a few scattered German troops wandering across the bridges heading into Carentan, but the longer we watched, the greater their number became. Finally there was a steady stream of troops crossing and we stood there powerless to do anything except pray for the Air Corps to show up. They never did. We watched the troop movement for better than three and a half hours and estimated their numbers at better than three thousand. These troops were the main body of the ones the five of us had attacked the day before and had been fighting with until the rest of the troopers arrived. If they had known that there were only five of us at the beginning, they would have sent a detail out and walked all over us.

After digging in and setting up a good line of defense, some of us set about looking over the area and the German equipment that was strewn about. An apple orchard was just over to our left and the Krauts had had a large wood-burning stove and some tables set under the trees, evidently a battalion mess. Two plucked ducks lay on a small table next to the stove and a dead American trooper lay on the ground in front of it, still in his harness. They must have killed him when he hit the ground. Another trooper lay spread-eagled on a picnic style table, also in his harness. He had died of several knife or bayonet wounds in his chest and belly.

Dead cattle and horses littered the entire area and some of them were starting to bloat up, the gas escaping from their wounds and natural openings giving off an odor that sure didn't blend with the scent of the apple blossoms on the trees. Phillips wanted to look at some motorcycles next to the road, but I was more interested in a line of small, horse-drawn wagons pulled in close under the protection of a high hedgerow. The wagons contained German paratrooper uniforms, packs and weapons, from which I picked a new P-38 pistol that had never been fired. In fact, it was still encased in grease. To the victors go the spoils, goes the old saying, and we were all busy looting the wagons, packs and enemy dead for watches, weapons or just plain souvenirs.

Night was coming on so we all returned to our foxholes and strung grenades out front, tying them to the bases of small twigs. Then, pulling the pin most of the way out, we ran a wire from the pin out about fifteen feet and tied the other end to another twig. This way, if anyone walked through and kicked a wire, the pin would be pulled all the way out and the grenade would do the rest. After stringing dozens of these out the entire length of our defense we settled down, two men to the foxhole, and took turns sleeping and watching. But before settling down for the night I made one last trip to the Kraut kitchen. I took several loaves of black bread, a couple of tubes of cheese, which were in tins, like grossly oversized tubes of toothpaste, a can of ersatz coffee, two cans of ersatz cigarettes and the canteen of water from the dead trooper.

Returning to the foxhole we tried cutting the bread and finally ended up doing the job with the machete I carried. It was the hardest stuff I ever tried to chew. The cheese wasn't bad, but the ersatz coffee and cigarettes tasted like hell. We threw them away.

Phillips said it was bad luck to take water from a dead man.

"Why?" I asked. "He doesn't need it now and if he were alive and I asked him for a drink he would give it to me. If I get killed you can have my water."

"Never mind the water," he said, "I've got first dibs on that shiny .45."

"I've got seconds if you get killed, Phillips," put in Benson.

Everyone had a place in line to inherit my nickel-plated .45 automatic, if and when I got killed or my successor in line got killed.

Just before dawn the grenades started going off. We cross fired with machine guns from either end of our company sector and the riflemen laid down a field of fire straight out. The lead really flew for a few minutes, but not one shot came in our direction from the enemy, so we ceased fire and waited, eyes straining, at the edge of the foxholes for the light to get strong enough to see by. When at last we could see across the field, the sight that met our eyes was a large flock of sheep, shot all to hell and all deader'n hell.

A big stillness hung over everything this morning. I guess that both sides were regrouping and licking their wounds. The captain called me and ordered me to take a verbal message back to Regimental Headquarters in the center of St. Côme-du-Mont. I was to tell them of our strength, position and other vital statistics that couldn't be trusted to go out over the radio at this time. I started out alone, and once away from the men and the sound of their voices, there wasn't a sound of any kind. The shooting had stopped in this area and there was no sign of life, no birds, no people or troops moving through, not even a breeze to rustle the grass or leaves.

It was spooky walking through here and I kept looking around, half expecting to see something rise up from the hedgerows to leap on me. Maybe an enemy soldier had been left behind and was waiting in the underbrush for just such a chance as this to kill a lone American. A sweet sickly smell reached my nostrils, the smell of death. There was always this smell right after a kill, one which became even more rotten and decayed after the bodies had lain in the sun for a while. After this I was able to detect this smell even before a battle, and at times this odor came to me even when I came close to Krauts in heavy brush or in dark nights. I think the odor before a fight was more of a sixth sense than an actual smell.

I had come to the place where we had waged the heaviest part of the battle the day before. It was the enemy side of the road where the five of us had first made contact with the German outfit making their last stand on this side of the river. The road was littered with dead, human and animal alike. They were jammed so close together that when I tried to step between them my footprints were left in the congealed blood that lay like a thick dark gelatin on the pavement. Wagons had burned among the bodies, causing them to swell and burst open, spewing forth entrails from horses and soldiers alike. The five of us had accounted for more than our share before reinforcements arrived, but most of this carnage had been caused by the heavy artillery fire and the concentrated attack by all the troops.

The stench became stifling and the quiet so dense that it began to ring in my ears. I had no choice but to go on. Finally I took to stepping from body to body as if they were stepping stones in a river of gore. The bodies were so bloated that occasionally they gave out noises that sounded like groans. This gave me quite a start and made me look around wildly to see if one of the multilated things was rising up. It seems hard to believe but I walked for about a quarter of a mile stepping from body to body. When I finally came to the end of the carnage it seemed as if I had stepped from a world of darkness back into one of sunlight.

I followed the main street into the center of town, where I located the regiment command post and delivered my message to Colonel Bob Sink. As there was no return message, I headed for a walk around town after the Colonel dismissed me. I was walking down a side street looking over some young girls working around their yards and houses, when a barrel-chested Frenchman came out of a doorway. He held up a jug of wine and, calling, "Vive les Americains," offered it to me. I threw the rifle down on him, flipped the safety off and motioned to him to take the first drink. At first he didn't understand, but when he did,

he laughed, tilted the jug and took a long draught. I
watched him for a few minutes, and as he was still standing
after this, I took the jug and joined him. He thought my
actions were amusing and slapped me on the back. I continued wandering about town and had quite a few drinks
with other civilians, including a lot of young girls. But no
matter who they were, I always followed the same procedure, making them drink first. This was the first chance I
had to mix with the French people. The only thing that
really shook me was, every once in a while, the sight of a
young girl or woman answering the call of nature in broad
daylight, right out in public. Well, "when in Rome, do as
the Romans do," I've always heard. So whenever the need
arose after that I just went along with the French custom.

By this time some of the troopers were riding horses
left behind by the Russian cavalry. Some of them wore
their rifles strapped across their backs and carried pistols
on each hip, cowboy fashion. They rode through the back
streets and across fields searching for stray Krauts or snip-
ers. It's strange how many GIs hit by rifle bullets later said
they had been hit by a sniper. A sniper is a highly trained
individual who is usually left behind when an outfit has to
withdraw from an area. He is an expert on camouflage and
concealment and is an excellent shot. He usually picks a
spot from which he can watch and cover such things as
water pumps, holes, gateways, narrow approaches and
roadways, and hardly ever fires if there is more than one
person. He is not there to commit suicide, but rather to kill
a lone enemy whenever he can do it without getting spotted or caught. He usually has an escape route picked out

ahead of time in case things get too hot. We had had several men killed by such individuals, but the rest were either killed or wounded by plain ordinary enemy CLs. A sniper hardly ever just wounds a man. With a scope and a steady place to shoot from, he nearly always kills with the first shot.

Starting back in the general direction of the company area, I ran into a trooper carrying what appeared to be a Schmeizer with a long bent barrel.

"That's no good," I told him. "Why don't you get a good one, there's plenty of them around here."

"Hell, this is just the thing I need to keep from getting my head blown off," he said. Then he showed me that the burp gun was made that way and could actually shoot around corners. It wasn't worth a damned for firing straight ahead, but a man could stand next to a wall and with the 90 degree bent barrel shoot around a corner without showing himself. He fired a few bursts with it to show me how it worked.

"You can have it," I said. "I'll keep my M-1."

I finally ended up at a church that still had a steeple. This was rare in Normandy now, for most church steeples had been blasted down by our artillery because they were used as observation posts by the enemy. A graveyard was on the left side of the church and was held in place several feet above a small curved dirt road by a stone retaining wall. Facing the road on the opposite side of the wall was a small stone garage dug back into the dirt bank. It had been stripped of equipment by the Krauts, and now, because of its bunker-like construction, our medics had taken it over and were using it for a hospital.

I stepped inside to talk to some of the wounded lying on the floor. I might get some information on some of my buddies who were still missing. Before I could talk to any of them, a jeep roared up the dirt road with two tires shot flatter than cow pies. An oriental American doctor was bent low over the wheel and as soon as the jeep stopped he leaped out and called to the men standing around to give a hand in getting the four stretcher cases off. We looked at the two on the front. They were dead. So were the ones on the back. The ones on the back were shot up so bad that splinters of white bone protruded from their limbs and bodies. One of the men's intestines hung over the jeep's side and trailed on the dirt road. The red cross painted on the side of the jeep was spattered with their blood.

The doctor told us that he had picked them up near the bridges to Carentan. Before he could get back, four Germans had leaped from a hedgerow and started machine-gunning the wounded on the stretchers. He had tromped the gas to the floor and burned rubber in getting away from there, but not quickly enough to save the wounded. His tires had been shot flat as he sped away and the enemy had continued shooting at the back of the retreating jeep until he was out of sight. He told us that firing had broken out again in that area and begged us to help him find tires so he could return and help the wounded. Some of the men knew where tires could be gotten from wrecked jeeps and went for them on the double.

This was the end of my excursion and I headed back the same way I had come in the morning. Artillery was coming in now and landing everywhere, from our front lines clear back to the other side of St. Côme-du-Mont. Walking back along the road where the dead were so thick, I noticed a young German officer lying on his back. He was very young, handsome and well built. Out of some morbid curiosity, I lifted the bandage on his belly and saw that he had been shot squarely in the belly button. From the blood caked around the wound, he must have lived a long time after being hit. Well, that's T.S. as far as I'm concerned, I thought to myself. I went a little farther to the left and came to the place where Hagenbuch and I had shot it out with the Krauts and where Hagenbuch's body still lay in the ditch. Looking down from the bank, I counted twenty-seven dead Germans, and though these were the victims of my machine gun, the sight of Hagenbuch made this number seem small.

I cut across a field and came to another road. A trooper sat under a tree along the road's shoulder. He had a cigarette in his mouth and a lighter in his hand, but he made no move to light the cigarette. I walked over and spoke to him. Then I saw the bullet hole in his forehead. The man was dead. He had died so suddenly that his thumb still held the lighter trigger down, his right arm rested on his right knee, and the lighter was just a couple inches from the end of the cigarette. Not bothering to move him, I headed back to the company.

I arrived at the foxholes and found that the Krauts had made a small attack, a feeler's movement really, which had been dispersed quickly. Benson, Phillips and I were lying on the grass near our holes when Jackson's big frame swaggered toward us through the apple orchard. One look at the wide grin on his face told us he had something up his sleeve. When he reached us he asked, "How would you like to be rich?" We all agreed that we would and asked if he had found a fortune.

"Sure," he replied and produced a handful of crisp new French francs from his jump pants pockets. At two cents a franc the thousand franc notes added up to better than ten thousand American dollars. He handed them around and told us to keep them; there was plenty more where that came from.

After a little coaxing he took us to a shot-up truck. We looked in the back and found that it was loaded with French money. It must have been a German payroll truck. We all dug in and filled our pockets with as much money as we could carry, even though all we wanted it for was to show off in front of the other men. For we figured that it was German printed, and now that the Allies had landed and were liberating France, it would be worthless. I put a few francs in my wallet for souvenirs, then, along with the rest of my buddies, paraded around in front of the rest of the men in the company throwing thousands of dollars through the limbs of the apple trees and watching the wind carry it away. Some months later I showed my souvenir francs to a paymaster and asked him if they were any good.

"As good as gold," he replied.

For a minute I thought I was going to puke.

After the fling with the money, we were looking around for a little more loot when Thomas and I came upon a sloping hole in the ground used by a French farmer for watering his cattle. We walked down into it and found two dead Germans sitting upright against the wall. An artillery shell had landed in the center and the heat from the explosion had torn away their features. Their lips and ears were missing and the empty eye sockets looked black in the charred and wrinkled skin. The concussion had snapped their hands and feet off at the wrists and ankles.

"They sure are a mess, aren't they?" Thomas asked.

"They never knew what hit them," I replied, remembering my first night in the same kind of a hole and thinking how lucky we were that no shell had landed in it.

We were just about to climb out when I heard a low mournful groan. I asked Thomas if he were trying to shake me up.

"Hell no," he said, "I thought that was you."

We were still looking at each other when the sound came again from the right rear. For a full minute neither of us moved. Then as we turned and faced the corpses, one of them started swaying back and forth while the other groaned, louder this time. They must have been like this since our big attack the day before. How could they have survived the explosion of the shell, let alone live this long in their condition? There was only one thing for us to do for them.

"You take the left and I'll take the right," said Thomas.

We both took aim and fired at the same time, it was the least we could do for them. Returning to our positions we told the other men what we had found and they became quiet for a little while. I think they were wondering whether, if this should happen to any of them, someone would be as merciful as we had been.

We settled down on the edges of our holes again. We didn't want to get too far away, for the artillery was getting heavier and more frequent. Horses wandered about grazing. Some of them had bullet holes in them that had festered, and big green flies crawled in and out of the holes laying eggs or maggots. I munched on a hard K ration biscuit as I surveyed the field with its dead Germans and cattle. The cattle were now so bloated that their skin was stretched tight, and one had its legs pointed straight up toward the sky, its udders sticking straight out, like so many stiff fingers. Putrid stuff ran out of the openings. The smell was awful.

The Jourdan, the Douve and the Madeleine Rivers, along with myriad smaller channels and canals lacing the swamps and marshes, separated the cities of Carentan and St. Côme-du-Mont. A scattering of houses and buildings were built along the main road between the two cities, some of them on the water's edge near the bridges. Three bridges stood in a line along the Carentan causeway and all of them had to be traversed in sequence to get from one side to the other. Our lines were dug in the high ground just outside of St. Côme-du-Mont, but we maintained forward observation and listening posts in the territory between our lines and the river. I guess in World War I this would have been known as "no man's land," an area between two enemy forces not really held by either side.

Small groups from the German outfits that had pulled back across the rivers still pockmarked this piece of real estate, with its fields, hedges, trees, scattered farms and swamps. These holdouts and diehards harassed us and gave us a hard time whenever they could. But we were no slouches at dishing out this kind of treatment ourselves. Some of the troopers would prowl the hedges down to and into this area just to look for enemy O.P.s and strongholds. One trooper wore a brace of Luger pistols, cowboy fashion, and rode a white horse commandeered from the late Russian cavalry. He was with a group of us that was out foraging for wine, when we ran into a German machine gun in a house on the right side of the road, just this side of the first bridge. The gun opened up on us with long bursts and we hit the ditches on either side of the road, but the trooper on horseback spurred his mount, and yelling, "Hi Ho Silver!" charged the machine gun with both pistols blazing.

He rode within a few yards of the machine gun while it ripped long bursts around him and his mount, then, wheeling around, he dashed back to us and the safety of a hedgerow. I guess the machine gunner was too busy dodging pistol bullets to get in a well aimed burst at the trooper. We told him to cut it out or he was going to get it, but he said they couldn't hit the broad side of a barn and made two more charges against the gun. "How lucky can a man be?" I thought, as he made yet another run through the hail of bullets. It was unbelievable, but we all witnessed it. He turned, yelled, "Hi Ho Silver!" again and started back for another try. But this time the gun zeroed in and almost chopped the trooper in half as they shot him out of the saddle. The white horse ran past us and the last we saw of him, he was still going at a full gallop.

We tried several times to get down the ditch or around the back way to get at the machine gun, but it was too well covered and each time we barely got back with our skins. We finally said to hell with it. We would come back when we had a few more men to give us better cover. Returning to our positions we found that nearly all our men had returned or were accounted for. It was good to see Liddle, Gaddy, Sergeant Newton, Sergeant Impink and the rest of the men. Each and every one had a story of his struggles to get here through miles of enemy-infested land. And each story would more than fill a book such as this one.

One of the men told us he had landed in an enemy regimental area the night of the jump and hid in a hedge until daybreak. Sounds of hundreds of men moving about in the early morning hours made him burrow deep into the undergrowth. As it grew lighter he peered out and saw Germans falling out to stand in a chow line. They acted as if they didn't even know the invasion had started. What really surprised him was the fact that there were pretty young French girls, dressed and partly dressed, standing in line along with the German soldiers, waiting for their breakfast. Later that day excitement rose in the camp, and men started scurrying around and groups of them loaded into trucks and left camp.

"Why didn't you attack them," I asked with a serious face, but was really only kidding.

He looked at me with his mouth open for a moment, then said, "You go to hell. I'm not about to attack a couple of thousand Krauts and get myself killed for nothing. I waited until night and crawled away from there, real quiet."

Liddle was lying on his side chewing on a straw. He broke in, in his quiet way, and said that he, Benson and Jackson had attacked a couple of thousand Krauts. At first we thought he was kidding, but he insisted that it was the truth. Jackson and Benson hadn't said anything about it before, so we called them over and asked if it were true. "Sure," they said, "but it was all Liddle's idea."

The three of them had gotten together the first night and tried to find out where they were or at least contact other friendly troops, but everyone was so scattered that they had had no luck. At daybreak they started following a road and hadn't gone too far when they heard the sounds of a large motorized convoy coming toward them. They took cover in a hedge overlooking the road and watched as several Germans on motorcycles, acting as scouts for the main body, went past.

"What'll we do?" asked Benson as the convoy of trucks, half tracks, field guns, self-propelled guns, tanks, cars and troops came into view.

"You heard the man before we took off, didn't you?" said Liddle. "We're going to attack them."

"How are we going to do it?" put in Jackson.

"Just walk down there on the road and open fire," Liddle told them. "We've got the element of surprise on our side and we should be able to get a lot of them before they get us."

At Liddle's signal the three troopers slid down the bank and opened fire with M-1 rifles at the oversized convoy. Enemy troops leaped from the trucks and half tracks and deployed through the fields on either side of the road, while tanks and self-propelled guns backed up and maneuvered into defensive positions. Yells and orders passed up and down the long columns, and confusion reigned for several minutes, even with these veteran troops. Meanwhile the three troopers pumped round after round through the long rows of enemy troops before they had a chance to leap from the troop carriers. Liddle had just put his third or fourth clip in his M-1 when, in Liddle's words, "A man, sitting on a little bicycle seat on a great big gun, started turning a couple of little wheels and the big barrel started swinging toward us. Taking careful aim I popped him right off that little seat."

By that time other troops had gained the ditches and fields and opened up at everything in front of them.

"Come on," Benson yelled. "It's time to leave this place." The three troopers scrambled over the hedge and started running across the field toward a woods at the far end. Jackson said the machine-gun and rifle fire was so thick that he just knew that none of them would make it. He stopped, turned around, put his hands on his hips and laughed at the Krauts. Several machine guns opened up on him, and although he could feel the bullets snap by, not one of them touched him.

"Hell, if that's all the better they can shoot, I've got a chance after all," and he started out again, running like hell.

Liddle, Benson and Jackson, all three made it to the woods without a scratch and a couple of days later found their way to the outfit and were now sitting with us on the grass. As we lay there I thought to myself, I'm willing to bet that convoy was held up for better than two hours while they put out feeler patrols and scouting missions to make sure that it was safe to move again. I wonder what the commander of that convoy would have thought if he had known that his entire convoy was stopped by just three lone American paratroopers.

Jackson's face broke into a wide toothy grin. "I didn't

mind that so much, it was the landing I didn't like. My chute didn't open and before I even had time to reach for my reserve, my canopy caught on a tree. The tree bent over like a big whip or fishing pole, it bent clear over so that my feet barely touched the grass, then it came back up and held me about eight or ten feet off the ground. It was a hell of a job getting down, they must have dropped us pretty low."

Jackson's chute had pulled out of the pack tray but remained closed, a streamer. If it hadn't been for the tree snagging the canopy, he wouldn't have survived the fall.

Another trooper told me that he landed in waist-deep water. He waded to shore and made his way inland. There was no use looking for his buddies. He was the first man out the door and the water he landed in was the English Channel. His entire stick landed farther out in the channel and every one of them drowned. He said that he heard some of them call for help before they went under.

Johnson said, "Do you know that Colonel Turner is dead?" Colonel Turner was our battalion commander, a small man in stature, but all man and all officer. He came from Texas and spoke even slower than most people from that state. It made me feel that my lungs were running out of air just to listen to his long drawn out sentences. When visiting a company area nothing escaped his attention. It seemed as though he had eyes in the back of his head. We admired and respected all our officers, for they had to go through all the training that we did and under the same conditions. But there were still those who stood above the rest and commanded our greatest respect; Colonel Turner was one of these. The news of his death seemed unbeliev-able. Johnson went on to say that Colonel Turner had climbed aboard one of the first tanks to reach his group to guide the tank against a strong enemy position. He was standing in the turret, exposing himself from the waist up, in order to get a better view to guide the tank. A bullet struck him squarely between the eyes and he fell dead never knowing what hit him.

Suddenly our talk was broken up by incoming artillery and we had to take to the cover of our foxholes. Some of the foxholes left by the Krauts were elaborate affairs, as they had had the time to fix them the way they wanted. The sides were of woven wicker and the tops were covered by huge cement slabs that rolled back and forth on small metal tracks laid on either side of the hole. Shells were slamming into the field now and Screaming Meemies were shredding the air as they plowed their way from the six-barreled mortars to our lines. They never seemed to do great damage but they made the damnedest sound, like ten thousand wildcats fighting in a graveyard at midnight. They shrieked and screamed through the air, then hit the ground and exploded with such force that the concussion bounced men around like peas in a policeman's whistle. Every shell sounded like it was coming right down be-tween your shoulder blades and made you hug the ground until you felt you were part of the dirt itself.

Most of the grazing Russian cavalry horses had followed us when we had run for the foxholes. Now, looking up during the barrage, I saw a horse standing over me, ner-vously trampling the ground. His eyes rolled back in his head until nearly all the white showed. "Shoo," I said, "get away from here." He was standing so close that he threatened to break down the walls of my foxhole and come down on top of me. From where I was the horse looked twenty feet high.

After a while the barrage lifted and we came out of the holes again and went about our business of scouting, looting, cleaning weapons and consolidating our positions.

Thomas asked if I would like to go with him and Phillips to get some wine.

"Where's it at?" I asked.

"In a house down by the river," he answered. "I already got some from there."

He had picked up a big German motorcycle with side car and was using it to run around in. The three of us climbed on and headed toward the rivers. On the way Thomas told us that he had killed a Jap in full Japanese uniform. At first we thought he was kidding, but a little farther up the road he showed us the Jap's body lying in the ditch on the right side of the road.

"What the hell is he doing here?" I asked.

"Damned if I know," answered Thomas. "Maybe he's here on lend-lease from Japan to teach the Krauts how to camouflage; they're good at it, you know."

Later the men of the 506 were to run into more of these Japs and kill them. I still don't know their purpose in being there in Normandy.

We pulled up in front of the house that held the German machine gun and followed Thomas inside.

"You know, this house had a machine gun in it," I told the other two. "They almost killed our asses."

"I know," said Thomas, "they're still upstairs, so be quiet and don't drop any bottles."

"How come they didn't shoot when we drove up?" I asked. "Hell, I don't know, maybe they think we are their own paratroopers or maybe they're all asleep."

We each took an armload of bottles of wine and loaded them into the side car of the cycle. A couple of trips filled it. Thomas got on the bike and cranked it up, Phillips climbed on the seat behind him and I sat on the back of the side car facing the rear, with my legs wrapped around the spare tire to hold on and a tommy gun held at ready in my hands. Just as we started off a couple of Germans appeared at a window and started yelling. I fired a burst at them, but with the bouncing of the bike it was hard to get in a well-aimed shot. They jumped back from the opening for an instant, then a machine gun protruded and started firing at us. By this time we were racing wide open down the road, zigzagging in and out of large holes that had been blasted in the blacktop. It was all I could do to hang on, let alone return fire. Not being able to see the holes because of my backward position, I was nearly thrown off several times when Thomas swerved around them. We finally came to the apple orchard where the company was dug in and shared our wine with the other troopers. Water was hard to get. Even the public pumps that were working could not be trusted to give clean water. The men took to drinking wine, cider and champagne, which seemed to be plentiful in Normandy, in order to conserve what little water they still had.

By this time some Frenchmen had begun digging large pits to bury the dead cattle and horses. They used horses to drag the carcasses into the holes. Then they poured kerosene on the carcasses, burned them, covered them with lime and refilled the holes. The French also buried the German dead. Some of the graves were marked, some weren't. Most of the Germans were buried on or near the spot where they were killed.

We had a team called Graves Registration Team that followed us in. After everything had quieted down and our lines became fairly static, this outfit would move in, gather up all the American dead they could find, transport them back to a central cemetery and give them a decent burial. Some of the French were looting boots and clothing from the German dead. After all, why should a good pair of boots be buried when surely they could be used by someone? But it got to the point where after a fight these people would come out and loot the bodies while they were still warm.

Looting was a favorite pastime, even among the troopers. It was while I was busy at this occupation that I came across several sniper rifles. They were equipped with scopes and flash hiders. The mechanisms worked like glass. They were beautiful weapons and I longed to send one home for deer hunting after the war. This was impossible, so I took them one by one and smashed them against a tree so no one else could use them against us.

I was brewing some K ration coffee on a squad stove back in the company area when Colonel Sink arrived. After walking up and down our line of foxholes and staring across the river for several minutes, he maintained that the troops in Carentan were British.

"Colonel," some of the men said, "we've been watching

those troops all day and we know that they're Germans. We've even got a large pair of German binoculars on a tripod and have watched them put machine guns in several of the houses."

"Well, I've got to see for myself," he said. Then he picked Liddle, Creed and several other troopers as volunteers to go along with him into the city. One of them was a little Swede who spoke with such an accent that it was hard to understand him.

They all piled into a jeep, went down to the river and found a small boat to cross in. The second bridge had been destroyed. We watched through field glasses as they rowed across to the other side and with Colonel Sink in the lead they walked in single file up the main street into enemy lines. Suddenly all hell broke loose. Enemy machine guns opened up on them along with a hail of rifle fire. The troopers hit the ditch and in a crouched position started running back toward the river and our own lines. When they reached the river, Sink and a couple of troopers got into the boat and started back. Creed and the rest dove headfirst into the water and started swimming, diving from time to time to dodge the bullets that were sending small geysers and sprays of water up around them. All of them made it back to our side, got in the jeep and drove back to where we were waiting for them. Some of them were soaked to the skin, but all still carried their weapons.

"Goddammit," Colonel Sink said, "I could have sworn there were British over there, and I was going to shake Monty's hand."

Some of the troopers lay on the ground and laughed. Creed pulled out his cigarette pack, poked his fingers into the soggy mess, then started bitching. It was his last pack of cigarettes. He stalked around the group of men in squishy sounding boots and said, "You know, Colonel Bob actually thought he was going to shake hands with Monty." The Colonel had left by this time and was probably heading back toward St. Côme-du-Mont.

"I'm just glad we all got out of there in one piece," Creed said. "But right now I'm hurtin' for a cigarette, anybody got one?"

A couple of packs were donated to him and someone said, "You've got to hand it to Colonel Sink though. Most commanders would send a patrol out to find out what they want to know. Colonel Bob won't ask a man to do something he wouldn't do himself. You don't mind going out for someone like that, even getting shot at a little, if it's necessary."

The Fourth Division was moving by on the road now and we walked over to watch them go by. It felt good to know that someone else was going out in front for a while and do some of the fighting. While we were standing there watching, Phillips said, "That was some stunt that Jackson pulled the other day wasn't it?"

"I don't know," I replied. "What was it?"

"Well, there was a sniper somewhere in the hedges near town and no one could locate him. He killed a couple of troopers when they were alone. Jackson put on a couple of flak vests, one over the other, that he had gotten off several dead pilots in a field. Then he walked into the center of the field where the sniper was supposed to be and made out like he was looking for something on the ground while Wisniewski hid in a hedge to shoot the Kraut when he opened up at Jackson. The first shot caught Jackson just to the left of the breast bone, spinning him around."

"Why didn't you shoot?" he asked Whiskey.

"I didn't see him," Whiskey replied.

Jackson and Wisniewski were close friends and Jackson, along with the rest of us, called him "Whiskey" for short.

The second shot hit Jackson squarely in the chest, knocking the wind out of him.

"I see him," Jackson called, and he fired a shot that caught the sniper in the head, killing him instantly.

The Fourth Division had passed, so we moved back to our positions, settled down for the afternoon and got ready for the coming night. In the evening we lay on the edges of our foxholes, feeling secure now that other troops had moved out in front of us and the Krauts were on the other side of the river.

"Look there!" Phillips exclaimed.

A Stuka dive-bomber was coming down out of the sky. We could see it long before we could hear it. Diving at the bridges, it released a bomb, pulled up and scooted away in a sweeping turn back to its right. The bomb hit the marsh and mud and water flew in all directions.

"Boy, was that rotten," Phillips said. "He couldn't even hit the bridges. Did you see where that bomb landed?"

"Yeh, right where it couldn't hurt anything," I answered. Later that night we got word to move out. The Fourth couldn't make it across the river. We would have to take the city of Carentan.

We moved out just before sundown, following the same road the Fourth had taken earlier. It was dark by the time we reached the river. Across the black mirrored water stood the houses and buildings of Carentan. We knew the dark silhouettes held German soldiers, some of whom we had fought earlier and driven back here. Colonel Cole and two enlisted men had strung a rope, planking and a metal grate or fence across the span where the second bridge had once stood. In single file and about twenty feet apart, we moved the entire 506 across the flimsy construction behind Cole's outfit, holding onto the rope while sliding our feet step by step across the wobbly planks. Mortar and 88 shells were landing around the bridge and machine-gun fire was harassing us. Looking down, I could see the dark swirling water below. If a man were wounded and fell in here he wouldn't stand a chance. The moon wasn't out and the night was very dark. Huge marshes and swamps spread out on either side of the causeway leading into the city of Carentan. It was impossible to travel anyplace but on the road, which the Germans had zeroed in on with all their weapons.

While crossing the last bridge, several men were killed and more wounded by a heavy barrage of mortar fire. One man fell just in front of me. He lay doubled up, a geyser of blood shooting from his mouth and running back underneath him in a puddle. A huge iron fence stood across the roadway. One by one we had to squeeze through a small opening in its center while machine-gun fire sprayed it, sending sparks flying as bullets struck the pavement and metal. Watching the men go through, watching one fall every so often, put a funny feeling back in my stomach. This was like making a jump, the line getting shorter and shorter, the doorway closer and closer. Soon it would be my turn in this game of mass Russian roulette. I knew I was scared, but I kept going. Then it was my turn. Dashing through the opening, I suddenly felt strong. My body reacted faster, and I didn't feel the bumps as I dove headfirst into the ditch on the side of the road.

We lined up again in single file, each man holding onto the belt of the man ahead of him, and started on an angle to the right through the swamps and marshes. Most of us put our cigarettes in our helmets to keep them dry as some of the water was up to our armpits. We moved silently, slowly and carefully through the water until we came out on high ground. Even then we held onto each other's belts in the dark as we moved cross-country toward Carentan. Once the entire column stopped while the scouts slipped ahead and cut the throat of a lone German sentry standing guard by a gate in a hedgerow. The Kraut's body lay across the opening, and one by one, the men stepped over it. We came to a blacktop road lined with houses and spread out along it, hiding in hedges and ditches, waiting for the signal that would start the attack.

The first light of dawn appeared, making the air seem colder than it really was. Gradually the light became stronger and the false dawn gave way to the coming of daylight. Still we waited. Dew covered our helmets and weapons. A barn door just across the street slid open. We could see several Germans moving about, most of them in their shirt sleeves, some of them washing their faces in basins of water. Three others were butchering a cow that hung from the rafters.

"Wait, wait," the Colonel said, "wait till I give the signal, then give them hell." One of the men in the barn stood on a barrel and opened the cow's belly. The entrails dropped into a wheelbarrow standing under the carcass. Another soldier rolled his sleeves up to the elbows, took the wheelbarrow and pushed it around to the rear of the barn. A few minutes later he returned. The men who had been washing their faces had a fire going in a fireplace and had placed a large griddle on it. Word was whispered from trooper to trooper to get ready for the attack. Then, just as one of the Germans placed several large steaks on the hot buttered griddle, the Colonel gave the word. A volley of gunfire erupted from the hedges. The enemy never knew what hit them. They died where they stood.

We remained in the ditches to see what results our gunfire would bring. Nothing happened. It seemed impossible, but the Germans in the surrounding houses still didn't know that they were being brought under attack. A motorcycle with side car and two German soldiers came down the road in our direction. The sun was just glowing red on the horizon, glinting off some of the windows that still had glass in them. The cycle was in front of us when several troopers opened fire. The driver fell dead, and the bike spun into the ditch spilling the passenger on the wet grass. He scrambled to his feet and started running back down the road as fast as he could. Dobreck jumped over the hedge, yelling to him to stop, that he wanted to take him prisoner and wouldn't hurt him. The Kraut looked over his shoulder, saw Dobreck on his heels and put on a burst of speed that would do justice to a track star. It looked as though he might escape and warn his own people of our presence. We couldn't shoot for fear of hitting Dobreck. Some of the troopers were standing up now, yelling, "Go, Dobreck, go. Don't let him get away." Dobreck glanced around with sort of an apologetic look on his face, stretched out his long thin legs, closed the distance and smashed the German in the back of the head with the butt of his rifle, killing him. He came walking back toward us with his rifle over his shoulder, holding it by the barrel and looking a little dejected.

"I didn't want to hurt the man," he said. "If only he had stopped he would be a prisoner right now and still alive."

We moved out of the hedges toward the houses, and for the first time the enemy opened up on us, and the house to house fighting started in earnest. One platoon, running down a side street, came to a place where the houses thinned out just as a flight of American fighter planes came in low overhead. The planes swung around, came in low, straight down the road and strafed the hell out of the troopers. One man was killed, one wounded and a lieutenant had the musette bag shot off his back. The lieutenant pulled an orange panel from his pocket and stood in the center of the road waving for all he was worth as the planes started their second run. At the last second the lead plane pulled up, waggled his wings and led the rest of his flight toward enemy territory.

We cleared this section of town of all enemy troops and set up a good defense in case of counterattack. Returning to the barn we finished cooking the steak the Germans had started and along with some wine taken from a cellar, settled back for a good steak breakfast and a good rest. The bodies still lay on the floor. We didn't bother moving them.

The order came for us to reassemble. There were still some strong enemy positions in the high ground to the rear of town and we would have to get them out. We made the attack through the houses and out into hedgerow country.

Once in the hedgerows the artillery gave us close support, firing on a hedge or target while we ran toward it. When we got close enough to the exploding shells to be in danger of getting hit, the artillery spotter relayed orders by radio, and the fire lifted and started working the next hedge. Working in this leapfrog manner we gained hedgerow after hedgerow until we were in command of the high ground to the right of the city. Entering the side streets we searched the houses and made sure that all the enemy had pulled out of this sector. Then, with the machine gunners standing guard, the rest of us scattered under the hedges to grab a few minutes' rest.

The Fourth Division had moved across the river by now and were occupying some of the ground we had captured and were mopping up some of the enemy stragglers. Sergeant Newton sent me back to their area for K rations for our men. Other Airborne men were there picking up rations too. The officer in charge asked me how many men were left in my squad. I told him. We counted out the packages, put them in a box and I started out with them. While crossing the fields I came to a large rich-looking house. Several troopers were going in and out of the different doors in search of loot or something to drink. One man came out of a cellar door on the left just as I started to enter the one on the right.

"There's only cider in that one," he said. "This one's full of wine and champagne, help yourself."

The box I was carrying was only half full of K rations, so I finished filling it with magnums of champagne. Then I stuffed my large jump pants' pockets and picked up as many bottles as I could. My arms felt as though they were pulled out of their sockets by the time I got back to where the men were waiting. But I didn't drop one bottle. I would have let the K rations go first.

"Where the hell have you been? What the hell took you so long? Did you get lost or something? Forget where we were?" All these questions greeted me when the men saw me coming, but when I started throwing the bottles of champagne on the ground and told them to help themselves, they told me what a good man I was. Man, this was living, just like the Waldorf. Corks popped and foam ran down the men's arms as they lifted the bottles. It was hard as the devil to drink that stuff from a bottle. It kept foaming up in our mouths and coming out through our noses. The men finished eating and drinking and began to gather in front of a few houses on a street that dead-ended at the hedgerows.

We had finished our jobs and were waiting for the Fourth Division to relieve us and take over our positions. We were only supposed to be in combat 72 hours, but the time had run several days over that. Suddenly Boyd looked up and yelled, "There go some Krauts." The rest of us looked where he was pointing. "In back of the hedges, cutting on an angle toward the end of the road!" he exclaimed.

The Germans were bent over low, running with their heads almost touching their knees.

"Let's get them," someone yelled, and we started running down the road to intercept them. They had crossed the hedge and started down the ditch when we opened fire. Four of them fell. As we started past the four in the ditch, Boyd stopped long enough to bayonet each one of them.

"I'm not going to leave one of them behind to play possum and shoot me in the back," he said.

We came to the hedge where we had last seen the Krauts, jumped over it at the corner and started down the edge of the field after them. They had had enough time to set up a machine gun behind the hedge at the other end of the field. When we reached the center of the field they opened up on us. We all hit the dirt at the same time and returned fire with our rifles. I was about the third man back from the front of the line and could see the little geysers of dirt spurting up in the short grass as the bullets came toward us in a fast stitching path. "Look out!" I yelled and rolled to the right. Some of the bullets nipped the sleeve of my left arm as they passed. The men behind me rolled to either side and the burst of machine-gun bullets passed between them without touching a man. The man in front of me kicked me in the face now as he started crawling backward. I think it was Dobreck.

"Move back," he said, "we'll never make it from here."

We all started crawling backwards so fast that we must have looked like a bunch of crawdads. I know that I nearly wore out the knees and elbows of my jump suit.

We made it back over the hedge, spread out and started firing on the enemy from behind it. I saw a Kraut poke his head through the undergrowth and, taking careful aim, I put a bullet through it. René and Creed were to my left along with several men, while the rest of the squad was strung out to my right.

"Oh my god," Dobreck exclaimed, "there's a pill box behind us."

Looking over our shoulders we saw a bunker that was so well camouflaged that none of us had noticed it. Dobreck and Robbie ran to it and up the sloping sides. It was only about forty feet away. They dropped hand grenades down a vent pipe in the top until they were sure that if there was anyone inside, they were dead.

Shells started dropping at the lower end of the hedge we were hiding behind. What with the enemy raking machine-gun and rifle fire at us from one side and our own artillery sending high explosive shells up the hedge at us from another, we didn't know which way to turn. The deadly barrage rained around us with such force that all we could do was to hug the ground. Smoke, dust and dirt were so thick that we couldn't see. It was even hard to breathe. Some of the men screamed. They were hit. But there was nothing we could do for the moment.

The barrage lifted for a few seconds, but we could hear more shells coming in.

"Let's get the hell out of here," someone yelled, and we started running back through the dust, smoke and explosions toward the road and the safety of the houses. Two men were carrying Robbie between them. Blood poured out of his side like a fountain and splashed down over his boots and onto the ground.

"How come it's so dark?" he muttered. "Why did the sun go down? It's getting darker."

The men boosted and hauled him over the hedge and

started toward the houses. René was dead and so was La-Rose. Several others had been severely wounded. Robbie died before we reached the houses.

An infantry captain had driven up in a jeep, parked near the houses we had captured, and was directing artillery fire by radio. Captain Davis ran to him and told him to stop the fire at once. It was killing our own men.

"There's not much I can do now," the infantry officer said. "I have to go through channels."

"The only place you're going is straight to hell," Captain Davis shouted as he grabbed him by the shirt and shoved a tommy gun muzzle in the soft part of his throat under the chin. "If you don't stop them right now I'm going to blow the top of your head off. Get busy."

The infantry captain grabbed the radio, and with sweat popping out on his face, issued orders for the shelling to stop. It stopped. Captain Davis threw the officer toward the back of the jeep and swore to himself. I kind of think the Captain would have liked to kill the dumb son of a bitch anyway.

One of our men was hit in the cheekbone with a wooden bullet. It had shattered into splinters, leaving a terrible wound. The man lay on the back of a jeep moaning and unconscious. I don't know whether he ever lived or died. Several of us walked back down the road, crossed several hedges and entered a large barn. Four large wooden barrels or vats were inside, each holding possibly several thousand gallons. We wondered what was inside, wine, cognac? "I'll find out," one man said. Holding his rifle at hip level he pumped three rounds into the first one. Liquid streams just smaller than a man's finger shot clear across the barn. Pulling his helmet steel and liner apart the man dipped the steel part into the streams, filled it and took a drink.

"Phooey, it's nothing but cider," he yelled, spitting the stuff out.

"Cider," echoed Liddle, and his face lit up like a kid's face in a candy store. Filling his helmet he started drinking his fill while the other trooper moved down the line tapping one vat after another with his M-1.

The screaming of artillery shells sounded and they slammed into the hedges around the barn. We left the place in a hurry to find better protection in the hedges. More shells came in, hit the barn square, and splintered wood flew everywhere. Some of the wood belonged to the vats. The next thing we knew, cider, thousands of gallons of cider, was flooding the hedges and ditches.

"The dirty rats, the lousy dirty stinking rats," Liddle raged. "They did that on purpose. All this time I've had to hunt for cider; now, just when I've found all I can drink, the Krauts blow it all to hell." Liddle was still grumbling as we walked back toward the houses and the group of men forming in front of them.

The Captain was bellowing orders. We were reforming for another attack. The infantry had bogged down. They couldn't move forward. We would have to act as shock troops again. We moved out in staggered formation, passed down through the Fourth's lines and headed through an apple orchard toward the low ground. Passing one foxhole I saw an infantry man holding his dead buddy in his arms and crying. This puzzled me, and I stopped for a minute to ask him what the trouble was.

"They've killed my buddy," he sobbed, with tears streaming down his cheeks. "But he can't be dead, we went through basic together; the medics have got to save him."

The man was dead all right, shot through the Adam's apple, and I told the infantry man so. "The only thing you can do for him now is leave him alone and help kill some of these Krauts."

Looking back I saw that he was still crying and holding the dead man in his arms. "He must be nuts," I thought. I have had buddies killed even in training and didn't feel like that. Not an hour ago Baranski, René, Bobbie and LaRose had been killed and several others badly wounded. I felt bad, but we couldn't sit around and cry about it. We had Germans to kill. While passing through the infantry's lines I noticed that a couple of them carried B.A.R.s. From the looks of them I was glad that we didn't have them in the Paratroops. Their fire power wasn't enough to compensate for their size and weight. Entering the low ground we looked up at the high ground with its natural fortresses of hedgerows and undergrowth and wondered how many enemy were up there and what they had in the way of weapons. Horse-drawn wagons stood in the first field, some of them canvas covered like the ones our ancestors are pictured in while crossing the western plains to California.

Troopers sneaked along the hedgerows, found spots that would be easy to cross when the signal was given and flattened out to wait. The 501st was supposed to be on our left flank. No one was on our right but hedgerow country and the enemy. Word was passed down from man to man to fix bayonets. We were going over the top. It sounded screwy, like something out of a movie. Bayonets clicked into place on the ends of the rifles. A short wait followed, then the command, "Let's go, over the top."

Grenades were thrown over the hedges and grabbing roots, small trees and brush growing out of the side of the hedge, we pulled ourselves to the top. Some of these hedges were well over twelve feet high. Then, sliding feet first, the troopers went down the other side to do hand-to-hand combat with the enemy. An officer, I had seen him before but didn't know his name, was running up and down the hedge yelling for the men to get moving.

"Get going, get moving over the top, hurry up," he yelled. He carried a carbine at port arms and was yelling at everyone in sight. Some men had found easier places to climb and had already made it over the hedge and were in the field. Others had denser, harder places to climb, so it took them a little longer. The attack did get off to a ragged start, but the men were doing their best.

"Get going there," yelled the officer, looking straight at me. I was near the top, pulling myself up by roots and trying to hold my rifle at the same time.

"Don't worry, joker, I'm ahead of you, so is everyone else, get your ass up here and go with us," I told him.

He stopped short, his mouth opened, then closed, then he started to climb too. Three enemy soldiers were on the ground just to my right, rolling around groaning. The troopers closest to them dispatched them with bayonets. Other Germans were already dead. The field was fairly large and surrounded with high hedges. Short grass about two inches high grew from corner to corner. There were no trees, ditches or gulleys for cover, just flat open ground to cross to the next hedge. Troopers were well scattered through the field, all of them doubled over or crouched as low as possible and running toward the other end of the field as fast as they could. I was crouched so low it seemed that my knees were driving on either side of my head. We all fired from the hip as we ran.

Halfway across, the enemy opened up on us with rifle, machine-gun, mortar and 88 shells. Our artillery, which had been pasting the hedges in front of us, lifted and started falling farther back in enemy territory. It was impossible to go back or to either side. We had to take the shortest route, straight into the enemy fire, to try and reach the safety of the hedge in front of us. The one that held the enemy. Men were being killed and wounded in large numbers, some of them horribly maimed, with limbs and parts of their bodies being shredded or shot away. I could feel the muzzle blasts of the men behind me as they fired from the hip. I was nearly as concerned about getting shot in the back by a fellow trooper as I was about the Germans in front.

Mortar shells blanketed the field. At least six machine guns were cross firing on us and that terrible 88 was shredding everything in sight. Bounding Bettys leaped into the air to sow their seeds of death on the ones who disturbed them. These were ingenious little devices of the enemy that were triggered when a man stepped on them. The bombs would spring into the air and explode about belly high. The explosion would send steel balls rocketing out in all directions, like the spokes of a wagon wheel. They were very effective. Men were being torn almost in half by them. We kept running straight at the enemy. It was like a dream—no, more like a nightmare. We were running for all we were worth, but standing still, getting nowhere. The hedge at the far end of the field seemed as far away as before.

We were being annihilated, our ranks disintegrating as we ran. Glancing at my comrades around and behind me to draw courage and strength from their presence, I saw that the field was being littered with dead, our dead. A trooper in front of and to the right of me was hit in the chest by an 88 shell. His body disappeared from the waist up, his legs and hips with belt, canteen and entrenching tool still on taking three more steps, then falling. Another trooper went to his knees, ran a couple of yards in that position, tried to gain his feet, stumbled and went down facefirst. Other men were falling, but at the same time others had gained the hedge and were lobbing grenades over it. We had been yelling and screaming like animals at the top of our lungs all the way. The Germans were falling back. But the next hedge was a duplicate of the first. Each time we gained a hedge, the enemy left a delaying force and pulled back to the next one and were waiting for us when we crossed the open fields with nothing but two inches of grass for cover. I don't know how many hedges we crossed in this bayonet attack but they seemed endless. Our attack finally slowed and came to a stop. We had to reorganize before going deeper into enemy territory.

Some of us took cover by a hedge to our left. Phillips was in front of me, Benson just behind. We lay there not knowing what to do next. Suddenly a strange smell came to our noses and wisps of a funny looking smoke crept over the hedges from our left. It clung close to the ground and moved slowly toward us. Phillips looked back at me. His eyes were round and wide. "Gas," he exclaimed. "What'll we do now?"

"Nothing," I said. "Just stay here and die I guess. I wish I had my gas mask now."

"So do I," said Phillips and Benson together.

They had been the first things we had thrown away. I would have traded anything for one of the thousands that lay scattered between the beach and here. The smoke reached us. At first I held my breath, but then realized that I couldn't do that for very long and took a deep breath, figuring to get it over with as quickly as possible. Nothing happened. The three of us looked at each other to see if we were really still here or if we had turned green or something. But everything was normal, except for the strange smelling smoke.

"It was just smoke," Phillips said. "That means they're probably moving. Wonder what they're up to?"

"I don't know," I said, "but we had better look around and find out what's going on." (Later I found that the smoke was laid down by our own artillery.)

The bushes up front rustled and moved. Someone was up ahead and I didn't think it was one of our own men.

"Stay here," I told the other men, "I'll go look," and I crawled forward on hands and knees toward the spot. Nearing the place, I waited, then inched forward again. In these thick hedges it was almost impossible to tell if an enemy was only a foot away. The leaves above me moved, parted and there stood a German with a potato masher in his hand. The cord had already been pulled from the handle. With a simple movement of the wrist he flipped the grenade, as though tossing away an empty beer bottle, and slid backward down the other side of the hedge out of sight. The whole thing had taken place in less than a fraction of a moment, faster than I could bring my rifle up to fire at him. The grenade landed in front of me. "I'll fix his ass," I thought, as I dropped my rifle and leaped forward to grab the grenade and throw it after him. I was still in mid-air with the potato masher just inches from my finger tips when the damned thing went off.

A ball of orange fire flashed in front of my eyes, thousands of small sand-like particles sprayed my face and hands, while a blast of heat, real furnace heat, hit me full in the face. My feet shot up past my face. In that last moment I didn't know whether they were still hooked onto my legs or not. Then total blackness.

Consciousness came back to me and I looked around to see that I was completely alone. Shells were exploding in the field, tracers lancing back and forth in all directions, but there was no sound. It was like watching a silent movie. I was deaf. Figures of troopers moved in the hedge across the field to my right. Checking for injuries I found that other than not being able to hear I seemed to be O.K. It was a miracle being alive. I have heard that sometimes a person can be just the right place in an explosion and live. A foot closer or farther away and the person is killed instantly. This is what must have happened to me, I must have been in just the right spot at the right instant.

Picking up my rifle and making my way across the field through small arms and shell fire, I joined the other men in the far hedge. Had I been able to hear the incoming shells and the crackling of bullets, I doubt that I would have attempted to cross that field. In the center of the field I could see the artillery and mortar shells erupting around me and feel the concussions of their explosions along with the soft slapping of air on my face as bullets passed close by. I never realized the intensity of fire in that field until later, when I had time to think back on it.

The Germans were attacking us from the right flank. A tank moved into view to my left, followed by Kraut infantry. A trooper fired a bazooka and struck it in the side. The turret swiveled and the 88 fired point-blank into the hedge where the trooper was lying. The exploding shell knocked him rolling end over end out of the hedge. He got to his hands and knees, shook his head, stood up, looked around, then started running away from the hedge. I thought he was running away from the fight. He ran a few yards, picked up his helmet from where it had been blasted by the concussion, put it on his head and returned to his position. A few moments later another bazooka shell rocketed from the hedge, struck the tank in the ribs again and this time the tank exploded with such force that I was lifted several inches from the ground.

Making my way to the left and past the bazooka man, I came to a corner in the hedges. A dead trooper lay there with a bullet hole in the center of his forehead. A sergeant to his right motioned for me to get down, then slipped over the hedge and disappeared on the other side. Hours seemed to go by before he returned, but when he did he carried a German machine gun over his shoulder and two boxes of ammo for it. He was wet, covered with mud and looked real mad. He said something to me that I couldn't hear. I pointed to my ears and told him that I was deaf, I couldn't hear my own voice. Still he talked, but gestured with his hands this time and I got the story that this was his buddy who had been killed and he had gone out to get revenge. He had crept through swamps in a wide circuit, found the machine gun, destroyed the crew with grenades and brought the gun back to use against the Krauts. There were no familiar faces among these men, so I asked the Sergeant where A Company was. He shrugged his shoulders as if he didn't know, thought for a moment, then pointed back across the field where I had come from in the first place. I thanked him and bending as low as I could, went racing back to the other hedge.

I went through a small white wooden gate in the hedge and found myself on a road. Troopers lay in the ditches on either side of the road. Many of them were dead or wounded. They filled the ditch so completely that there was hardly room for another man or body. A lieutenant with a carbine was kneeling in the ditch on the other side of the road studying a map. Rushing over to him and ex- plaining about my ears, I filled him in on the positions of the troops to the right and asked him to pass the word to his men so they wouldn't fire in that direction. He scrib- bled on a note that this was the right flank of the 501, that he didn't know where the 506 was unless it was up ahead somewhere, that the 501 had been a little slow in getting up here. He wrote further that he wanted me to go back to the other men and tell them of his positions so they could coordinate an attack.

I dashed back across the road and dropped into the ditch in front of the gate, waited until I saw that not too many shells were exploding in the field, then started through the gate. The gate suddenly spun around me several times, as though I were standing in the center of a merry-go-round. At the same time it felt as though a sledge hammer had struck me in the right arm and a shock like that of grabbing an electric wire flashed through my entire body. The ground came up hard and hit me several times before I finally rolled into the bottom of the ditch and lay on my back. My rifle lay against the bank. I tried to reach for it but my right arm wouldn't move. Taking my left hand and pulling my right arm up in front of me I could see the hole in one side of my sleeve and another one on the other side where something had passed clear through my forearm. I had been hit.

A dull throb came from my right side and I knew the bullet or shell fragment had entered my belly. I thought of the many rabbits I had killed with a shotgun and how their guts had been chopped to pieces by the shot. I could picture my guts lying in the bottom of my belly cavity, like someone had gone through them with an egg beater. I took my knife and cut the sleeve open. I was shocked to see that a chunk of flesh was missing from my arm. I could lay four fingers against the bone. A severed end of an artery hung about four inches out of the wound like a rubber tube, but no blood was coming from the wound at all. I poured sulfa powders in the wound, swallowed the sulfa pills, wrapped a bandage on as best I could and drank most of the water I had been saving. Someone grabbed me by the arm and looking up, I saw a medic bending over me, his lips moving in silent words. I told him to check my belly. I thought it was shot up pretty bad. He pulled my shirt and pants apart, laughed and told me there was nothing there but a big bruise. I could almost tell what he was saying by watching his lips move. What a relief!

Stripping off my harness and rifle belt, I felt something hot against the skin of my hip and feeling with my left hand, I found it was a piece of shrapnel, the one that had passed through my arm. The shrapnel had passed through my right arm, cut through eight rounds of rifle ammo in my belt, and cut through my jump suit, O.D.s and two belts. If it hadn't been for the rifle ammo absorbing the impact, I think the shell fragment would have gone clear through my belly.

A jeep stopped on the road. It was a medic jeep. The driver backed up and the first medic helped me into it. We picked up more wounded on the way back, four of them, all bad cases. Two were strapped to stretchers on the hood, while two more lay strapped to stretchers on the back. I sat next to the driver. The medic had two grenades in his shirt pocket, while I had my .45 and P-38 in holsters under my jump jacket. After seeing one medic jeep shot to ribbons, I didn't want to go down without a fighting chance. We made the run toward the bridges amid shell bursts and a few long range machine-gun bursts. As far as I could see none of them came too close, but I noticed that the driver hugged the steering wheel so close that his eyes were level with the hood. It was dark as we neared the bridges and drove between some houses scattered along the road.

Someone had built a heavier temporary bridge in place of the rope and plank we had used in getting over here. It was a makeshift affair but looked fairly sturdy. It had been built under sporadic fire by small arms and 88s. Whoever did it did a good job, considering that they had had to work out in the open over the water and as perfect targets for the enemy. The steel gates had been removed; it was a clear run across the rivers to the other side. The driver stopped back a ways from the bridges, motioned for me to hold on, then tromped it to the floor and the jeep shot forward. The Krauts must have heard the high whining of the engine, for artillery shells started landing around the road ahead and on either side of the bridge. Hearing had returned in my left ear, so that I could hear the shells coming in now and even hear a man talking if he spoke a little loud. We made it O.K., passed the house where Thomas, Phillips, and I had gotten the wine and went all the way back to a checkpoint.

A tent had been set up alongside the road and wounded men were being checked by a doctor before going back to a hospital. But I don't know what the purpose of this was, for the doctor in charge, a lieutenant colonel, was a fat man who did nothing but sit behind a desk and check wounded only if they could walk into the tent. The bad cases lay out on the litters, but he didn't go out to see them. When he looked at my arm, without taking the bandage off, he noticed the pistols in my holsters and asked me for them.

"Sorry, sir," I replied, "but I'm not giving them up to you or anybody."

He argued the point, saying it was the laws of the Geneva Conference and that I was compelled to hand them over to him.

"If you're captured in that jeep with those pistols, the Germans could shoot you."

"They'll do it anyway," I said. "Did you ever see what Krauts do to paratroopers they get their hands on? If they want this boy, they'll have to do it the hard way. Besides, if it is against the law, I'll have a better chance to get rid of them at the last moment in a moving jeep at night than you will if you're captured here in a hospital tent."

He didn't answer but asked if he could just look at the nickel-plated .45. Dropping the clip out and racking the shell out of the chamber, I dropped the gun on the desk in front of him. At the same time I pulled the P-38 from its holster and holding the muzzle chest high but not quite at him, I said, "Sir, the only way anyone will get that gun is off my dead body."

He handed it back to me and told me to get the hell out of there and back on the jeep.

The jeep driver was waiting. We had been held up too long. The stretcher cases needed attention. We must have traveled eight or nine miles before finally coming to a group of large tents that were painted with large red crosses and lit up with searchlights. Tent flaps were rolled up and doctors were operating in almost every tent. Nurses were moving about with expressionless faces under the doctors' commands and still other nurses hurried about with large pots of black coffee. Some of these doctors and nurses had been working without sleep for three and four days. I don't know how many men owe their lives to these hard-driving people.

A young doctor with haggard features had just finished at an operating table. He pulled his mask down, wiped his forehead with the back of his hand and hurried toward us.

"Any belly or chest wounds?" he asked.

"Yes sir," the medic replied.

"Then bring them in first, and hurry," ordered the doctor. Everything was lit up so bright, it was hard getting used to seeing lights again. One of the tents to our left was dark though, and I soon saw why. One of the men in our jeep had died on the way here and the medic and another man took him by either end and placed him on a pile of dead bodies beside the tent. There was no more room inside. It was full.

The doctor asked how long the man had been dead and where his wounds were. He had been hit in the upper left arm and evidently had bled to death on the way. He hadn't been dead for more than a few minutes, for I had seen him moving not too long ago. The doctor ordered that he be brought inside and put on a table. I stood just outside the tent and watched as people started hurrying around under his commands. Bottles were placed head high on metal rods on either side of the body and needles on long rubber tubes stuck in his veins. Two nurses placed small bags on the body after pouring small amounts of water in them, apparently to generate heat to warm the body. Then the doctor stuck a large needle in the dead man's chest. "If he wasn't dead before, he is now," I thought. Then, with artificial respiration and other workings I didn't understand, they actually brought the man around. He was brought back from the dead.

I was put in a ward with other walking wounded and fell into a deep sleep on a canvas cot. It was morning when I awoke. They gave us something to eat after checking to see if anyone had belly wounds. Later a large group of us were moved to the beach and loaded onto LSTs. The sailors told us we would have to wait until the tide came in before we could pull off and sail for England. Walking up to the deck I gazed back at Utah beach and the high ground overlooking it. Some of the German pill boxes were made to look just like summer cottages, painted shutters and all. I noticed other pill boxes, gun emplacements, strong points and vantage points of the enemy on and behind the beaches. The men of the Fourth and other units must have had a hard time fighting their way through these fortifications.

About fifty yards from the edge of the water was a small puddle, about twenty-five feet in diameter. It didn't look more than a few inches deep, but sticking up out of the center was about a foot of turret of an American Sherman tank. I don't know whether the crew was still in it or not. Maybe the Graves Registration Team had removed them by now. I also wondered if the tank had fallen into the hole or whether it had sunk after leaving a landing craft and the hole was caused by the water eroding the sand from around the heavy steel monster. Several other tanks were in shallow water, their canvas water wings torn and shredded. These were the type of tanks that were supposed to swim ashore with the aid of rubberized canvas walls built up around the deck. Bullets and high waves had torn the canvas apart. Very few, if any, had made it to shore.

I happened to look down into the water. It was filled with countless thousands of jellyfish. One could see a fluorescent purple, four-leaf clover design in the center of their jellied bodies. Leaning on the rail, I wondered where they had been during the bombing and shelling. And, if it were possible for them to think at all, what they thought of the higher form of life—the human race.

Returning below deck, I was assigned a place next to several wounded Germans. The one next to me had been machine-gunned through the legs and was in a cast from his waist down. There were no cots. We lay on the floor or leaned against the walls as best we could. The badly wounded lay in the center of the floor. A wire stretched the length of the hold over them, high enough so that men could freely pass under it while caring for the wounded or going about their duties. Bottles of plasma and glucose hung from the wire with long rubber tubes leading to the patients under them.

Night came and with it the Stuka dive-bombers. They droned about us in the dark like a bunch of mosquitoes looking for their prey. Suddenly several of them started screaming their way down. They had found us. Searchlights went on, stabbing long columns of light crisscrossing in searching patterns in the black skies above. Antiaircraft went into action and possibly diverted the bombers a little, but didn't stop them. One after another they came in, their screams getting louder and louder on the way down. It seemed as if they would never end their run. But finally the bombs started dropping. First one, then another. The ship would rock gently one time and violently the next as the bombs landed at a distance, then up close.

One bomb dropped in between our ship and the next one and for a moment I thought our ship was going to turn over. The Kraut next to me spoke in broken English, "Breaks the boat, I can't swim."

"That's too bad," I told him. "With those casts on your

legs you can walk on the bottom till you get to shore. You should have thought of things like this before you started the war."

Another Stuka came screaming out of the dark skies, and we knew by the sound it would be close. The Kraut started trembling and covered his face with his arms. The thought of this superman lying here shaking like a scared rabbit started me laughing. I kept laughing even after the bomb went off on our port side. A perfect bracket. If they could land one in the center, we would all go to hell together, the fast way.

The mad screaming of the dive-bombers finally slowed and came to a stop. As the planes droned off into the distance the antiaircraft stopped firing, and soon all became quiet again. I smoked a cigarette down halfway, crushed it out and fell asleep. How long it was or what time we pulled out I couldn't say but I did wake up when the ship started moving. We weren't allowed above deck now, so I moved about with the other walking wounded, helping the ones who were wounded so badly they couldn't help themselves.

The trip back across the Channel was smooth and uneventful, and for those of us who were not seriously wounded it was almost like a pleasure cruise. Arriving in England, we came to a stop bow first against the docks; the huge bow doors opened, the ramp was let down and the walking wounded left first. English people, military and civilian alike, lined the water's edge. They waved to us, said encouraging things and some had tears streaming down their cheeks. Somehow it made me feel as though my own mother were standing in the crowd.

We were taken first to makeshift hospitals, where some of us spent a day or two, then we were shipped to regular or general hospitals. Nurses kept giving me shots and pills every time I turned around, and to this day I can't recall how the trips were made from the LST to the field and general hospitals, whether by truck, train, bus, ambulance or jeep. I do remember very clearly walking into the hospital, the 216 General just outside Coventry, and following the ward boy down a maze of halls and into a ward filled with non-combat patients.

One bed at the very end of the ward was empty, and the ward boy told me to take it and get undressed and ready to take a bath. It must have been around the 17th or 18th of June, and I still hadn't washed since we made the jump. There was never the time or opportunity for such a luxury even in the field hospitals. My jump suit was torn and grimy, I needed a shave and still wore my fire-blackened helmet, force of habit I guess. The ward boy cut my jacket and shirt from me and helped me off with the rest of my clothes. He didn't touch the bandage. It was the same one I had put on when I was hit.

Two doctors came in followed by a nurse with a tray of instruments and bandages. They cut the old bandage off, and when they pulled it from the clotted wound the blood poured like water from a fountain, spilling over my legs and onto the floor. It was the first time it had really bled.

"Don't worry about it," one of the doctors said. "The ward boy will mop it up."

After a thorough examination they rebandaged the arm, told me they would be able to fix it just like new and left.

One of the patients in another bed asked me if I had taken part in the invasion.

"Yes." I answered.

"Here," he said, and threw me an orange.

I didn't want to take the man's last orange, but he insisted and said that he wished it were more. All of the men in that ward treated me like a king. They were a good bunch of Joes. The one who gave me the orange said that I was the first combat man he had ever met.

Things went on normally, for the next three days, with patients kidding each other, and some going for operations, others leaving for their outfits. The third day a large group of wounded came in and were taken to another section of the hospital. One of them was a young sailor. His left hand was gone at the wrist.

I visited another paratrooper in another ward. He constantly smoked cigars and was in a cast from the waist down.

"I guess you won't be jumping for a while," I said.

"Hell no. I can't even turn over; it takes four nurses to do the job."

The fourth day came around and the doctor who had originally looked at my wound brought in another doctor and introduced him to me as the one who would do the operating.

"I thought you were going to do it," I said.

"No," he replied, "this man's a specialist."

They didn't give me any breakfast that day, no lunch, then no supper. I was just getting used to eating again and now they were trying to starve me to death. Later that afternoon a nurse gave me a shot and I took a bath. They were going to operate in less than an hour. The ward boy wheeled in a table and helped me on it for the trip to the operating room.

"Wait a minute," I told him, "there's something I've got to get from my bed."

He wheeled me back and I recovered the two pistols that I had secreted there when I first arrived. The ward boy's mouth opened as though he were going to say something, but he thought better of it and wheeled me into the operating room without speaking.

The three nurses asked me all sorts of questions while they worked. All three were from Detroit. At least that's what they said. They laughed when I asked them if they knew where Rouge Park was. One of them said she could only find her way around Rouge Park at night. This seemed hilariously funny to me and I couldn't help but laugh uncontrollably even when they tied my arms to boards sticking out from the sides of the operating table. The doctor came over and talked to me a little. Then, when he pulled the sheet covering my body down to my waist, there lay the two pistols in plain sight. I told him the .45 was from my father and the P-38 was the only souvenir I had managed to keep from combat. He stood there looking at me for a moment, then returned to a tray filled with instruments. A nurse put a needle in my left arm. It was attached to a rubber hose and a bottle hanging from a stand.

The nurse told me to count from ten to one. I got to eight and went under. That was about six in the evening.

When I awoke it was morning, back in my own bed and ward, everyone was eating breakfast. I felt something slide from my belly and, looking under the sheet, I saw the two pistols. The doctor had made sure I still had them. The doctors had been treating my ears every day and I could hear pretty well now. They said it would be just a matter of time and they would be as good as new.

"Where's my chow?" I asked.

"You don't get any this morning," the ward boy said as he was gathering up the empty trays.

"Like hell I don't," and getting up I started for the mess hall at the other end of the hospital. The floor didn't want to stay still. It kept moving about. I staggered down the main hall and ran smack into the nurse on duty in my ward.

"Get back in bed," she ordered.

"Not till I get something to eat."

She tried to wrestle me back into bed, but I was determined to get something to eat. She finally promised to get me a tray if I would return to bed and behave. I promised and she kept her word and brought me a tray of scrambled eggs, bacon, toast and coffee. It tasted so good that I asked for seconds, but she refused and said that I would have to wait for lunch.

Every day when the doctors arrived for their morning inspection the ward boy would yell "Attention," and all the patients who were able would leap to their feet and stand at attention beside their beds. After the doctors made their rounds the patients were allowed to return to their beds and continue getting well.

One day the nurse chewed me out after the doctors had left.

"It's only your arm that's hurt," she said. "*You* can stand at attention with the rest of them."

"Like hell," I told her. "I came here to get well and I'm sure as hell not going to do it by jumping up and down every time an officer walks in here. Everybody around here is an officer, even the nurses. I would be jumping up and down all the time. Now don't ask me again."

She got pretty mad and walked out of the ward, but left me alone to do just about as I pleased after that.

On their daily inspection tour the medics changed my bandage and swabbed out the translucent liquid that formed in the wound between the stitches. They told me that was new flesh growing in the wound and the reason they cleaned it out every day was to allow it to heal from the inside out and not leave a large indentation in my arm. One of the doctors also told me at this time that they had transplanted an artery from a dead man into my arm. I don't know if this is true or not, but an artery does lie just under the scar tissue.

The Fourth of July rolled around. That night we watched fireworks and were served ice cream on the lawn outside the building. A large number of English people were there to help in the celebration. A few days later, dressed in class A uniforms, a group of us stood at attention before the flag in front of the hospital and received our Purple Hearts. After the ceremony I walked into the main lobby and mailed mine home.

A few days later the doctor called me into his office, looked the scar over closely, and pressed on it with his fingers. Then he handed me a pair of scissors and told me to cut and pull the stitches. I did the first one gingerly. It didn't hurt, so I went through the rest of them like an old pro. Two days later they gave me traveling papers, a ration card and meal ticket, took me to the rail station, wished me luck and told me to return to my base camp. Arriving at Aldbourne, I walked through the village square. It was almost deserted. A few civilians turned to look at me. I was the first of the outfit to return.

I stood for a long time in the courtyard. It was deserted. No noise, no troopers hustling about, no one doing close-order drill. For the first time in many months I felt a deep loneliness. Opening the door of stable 13 was like opening the door of a tomb. Memories flooded my mind. I wondered how many men were still alive. The only thing to do was to keep busy, so I gathered up all my dirty laundry, went to the wash house, and scrubbed everything clean by hand. Returning to the stable I ate some fish and chips purchased earlier in town and went to bed.

Next afternoon when I awoke from a nap the sun was shining bright and a great racket came from the center of town. It was the outfit. The men had come back. Pulling on my O.D.s I ran toward the gate and halfway across the courtyard I saw them. They came running, yelling and laughing like a bunch of kids on a picnic. Phillips, Benson, Liddle, many others, all of them laughing, some with arms around each other. They were home. My buddies saw me and stopped. Phillips' mouth opened. Finally he said, "You're dead, we saw your body."

I told them how I was wounded, said that I had arrived here yesterday, done my laundry and was very much alive.

Back in the barracks they told me that after they had seen me hit with the grenade they had gone on through with the attack. The Germans counterattacked and a hell of a battle took place in a field near the Carentan road. They held their ground and the Germans fell back. This had been their last big fight. After they had established static lines and dug in, they had wondered if I were really dead or just wounded and had returned to what they thought was the spot where I had fallen. Along with Sergeant Impink they had found a body that looked just like me. It had been almost cut in half by machine-gun fire. I was officially reported killed in action. A telegram was being prepared, along with others, to be sent home to the parents. Captain Davis told me to take a jeep, go to Regimental Headquarters and stop the telegram going to my parents. At Littlecote Manor I had to sign three copies of a statement saying that I was still alive. They wouldn't just take my word for it.

Returning to the barracks I sat with my buddies and we talked. We talked of many things that night in stable 13. Of those who were dead, wounded or still missing. Some of the wounded had been sent back to the States and would never again rejoin us. Some of the wounded would heal and come back to the outfit as I had done, to make other missions, some to be killed or wounded later. Very few of us lived or stayed whole to make all the missions with the regiment. Some of the missing would remain missing forever, their whereabouts known only to God. We talked of the bayonet attack in the hedgerows and fields near Carentan. So many men had died there charging into the muzzle blasts of the 88s, the blanketing explosions of mortar shells and the heavy cross firing of rifles and machine guns that we came to call this place "The Battle of Bloody Gulch."

A couple of days after the outfit had returned we marched to Regimental Headquarters and there, in an obscure field, with our outfit on the right side side, and the troop carrier command on the left, General Ike delivered a message that never made headlines. First he complimented us on our execution of orders and the taking of all objectives on or before the given deadline. Then he chewed the troop carrier command out for scattering us all over hell's half acre, dropping us at dangerous altitudes and dangerous speeds. He ordered us to do a left face and the Air Corps a right face. Then he told the men of the Air Corps to take a good look at us.

"These are the men you carried in," he said. "A lot of their buddies will never return because of the way they were dropped. We are going in again, and when we do, I want every pilot to be able to look me square in the eye and truthfully say, 'Sir, I dropped my men, when, where and how they were supposed to be dropped.'"

After the speech and ass chewing we held formal ceremonies honoring our dead. I feel from the bottom of my heart that the troop carrier command did pull a big snafu in Normandy, but many times since then they have made up for it. I have witnessed pilots holding their crippled planes on course while the troopers cleared out, then die in the flaming wreckage. I have seen fighter pilots attack and drive off enemy planes that were trying to get close enough to bomb and strafe us when we were caught flat-footed in the middle of an open field with no cover. We've got the greatest Air Corps in the world, bar none, but the men are only human, like ourselves, and should be allowed one mistake. They have more than made up for it a hundred times over.

We returned to camp and received nine days' furlough, after which we settled down to build our strength back up to combat readiness. We were green before Normandy, but we had been baptized in fire and were ready and able to take on anything the Nazis could throw at us. We of the Airborne had captured and held all the ground from Ravenoville to Pouppeville, from Herbert to and including Carentan. This just about covered all the ground the entire width and depth behind the Utah beachhead. For this, the 101st Airborne was the first entire division to receive the Presidential Unit Citation.

We had other missions after this. By the time the war was over, the 506th was to suffer over 350 percent casualties. Every stable in A Company, with one exception, was to have men missing, either killed or wounded, some of the wounded returning home immediately, others much later. The exception was stable 13. Stable 13, the one occupied by Phillips, Benson, Liddle and myself, was the only one that had all its men return home after combat.

AFTERWORD

The 101st Airborne Division was activated on 16 August 1942 at Camp Claiborne, Louisiana, at the same time the 82d Airborne Division was activated. This dual activation came about by the splitting in two of the most promising infantry division in the U.S. Army at that time, the 82d Motorized Infantry Division, which had just completed its basic training under Commanding General Omar N. Bradley.

As the newly formed 82d began its career as the "All American Airborne division," the 101st began its new life and career as the "Screaming Eagle division," a number and name resurrected from a famed Union Civil War division. The officer charged with command of the fledgling Airborne was none other than Brig. Gen. William C. Lee, the "father" of the American airborne. It was General Lee who, for many years, had advocated airborne troops in the American military and had fought long and hard to get the Airborne established and off the ground.

The day following the activation of the 101st Airborne

Division, General Lee, in his first General Order Number One to his division, included a message which was to prophesy the honor and glory which was to become the 101st. "The 101st has no history, but it has a rendezvous with destiny. Like the early American pioneers whose invincible courage was the foundation stone of the nation, we have broken with the past and its traditions to establish our claim to the future. Due to the nature of our armament and the tactics in which we shall perfect ourselves, we shall be called upon to carry out operations of far reaching military importance, and we shall habitually go into action when the need is immediate and extreme."

The men of the 101st Airborne kept that "rendevous with destiny" and built the history of which General Lee spoke that first day. The paratroopers of the 101st set the standards and set the records that military the world over has unsuccessfully attempted to emulate and match to this day.

The Screaming Eagles first proved to the world its worth in battle on the shores, fields, towns, and cities in the hedgerows of Normandy. Well trained and of high morale but yet untested in combat, the paratroopers and glidermen descended through the darkest of nights to lead the way in the largest air and seaborne invasion the world had ever known on 6 June 1944 into Normandy to breach the walls of Hitler's "Festung Europa," Fortress Europe.

Eaglemen were baptized in fire, bathed in blood, maturing in first battle to strike unbridled fear in the hearts of the super race. From that night on the Germans would call the American paratroopers, "Butchers mit big pockets," referring to their skill in battle and the large pockets on their jump suits. The men of the 101st Airborne did not die quietly, but violently, turning the war back on its creators. We fought many battles after Normandy. During the Battle of Market Garden to liberate Holland, the 101st set an American military record for troops being on the line in constant combat without a break longer than any other troops in our history.

After Market Garden the 101st Airborne was rushed without warning or preparation to hold Bastogne, with its critical seven road network vital to the German cause in their major thrust, quickly named the bulge, in the German bid to split the Allies and possible victory, or cause at least an armistice, rather than total defeat.

There was no rest for the Airborne. Every front in every major battle area that felt fear of threat sent for the 101st and its expertise in battle to bail them out. As a result, the 101st Airborne became the only division in U.S. history to fight actively in three battle areas under three commanding generals, all within the short span of only sixty days. We fought in Holland under Field Marshal Montgomery. On being relieved from battle there the 101st was rushed into combat at Bastogne in the Battle of the Bulge under Gen. Omar Bradley. And again, when the Germans struck out with another threatened breakthrough in American lines in Alsace in Operation Nord Wind, the 101st was rushed in to serve under General Devers to successfully stem the Nazi advance in that area.

Our battles continued into the Ruhr Valley to aid Patton in his stalled breakthrough there. The 101st mounted several Rhine river assaults across Germany all the way to and through the Black Forest, through Bavaria and into the mountains of Austria, to become the first troops to march into Hitler's home, liberating several concentration camps with their gas chambers, ovens, and places of torture and horror.

In the the end the 101st Airborne was to become the only division to be awarded three U.S. Presidential Unit Citations and become General Eisenhower's personal honor guard.

At its conception and activation, the 101st Airborne had no history, but it had a "rendezvous with destiny." We kept that rendevous with destiny, and we gave it a history.

ABOUT THE AUTHOR

Donald R. Burgett lives in Howell,
Michigan. He is the author of *Seven Roads
to Hell*, *The Road to Arnhem*, and
Beyond the Rhine.